T0356422

Best Easy Day Hikes
Colorado Springs

Help Us Keep This Guide Up to Date

Every effort has been made by the author and editors to make this guide as accurate and useful as possible. However, many things can change after a guide is published—trails are rerouted, regulations change, facilities come under new management, and so forth.

We appreciate hearing from you concerning your experiences with this guide and how you feel it could be improved and kept up to date. While we may not be able to respond to all comments and suggestions, we'll take them to heart, and we'll also make certain to share them with the author. Please send your comments and suggestions to the following address:

Reader Response/Editorial Department
64 S Main St.
Essex, CT 06426

Thanks for your input, and happy trails!

Best Easy Day Hikes Series

Best Easy Day Hikes
Colorado Springs

Fourth Edition

Stewart M. Green

FALCONGUIDES

ESSEX, CONNECTICUT

FALCONGUIDES®

An imprint of The Globe Pequot Publishing Group, Inc.
64 South Main Street
Essex, CT 06426
www.falconguides.com

Falcon and FalconGuides are registered trademarks and Make Adventure Your Story is a trademark of The Globe Pequot Publishing Group, Inc.

Distributed by NATIONAL BOOK NETWORK

British Library Cataloguing-in-Publication Information available

Library of Congress Cataloging-in-Publication Data available

ISBN 978-1-4930-8111-0 (paper: alk. paper)
ISBN 978-1-4930-8112-7 (electronic)

♾™ The paper used in this publication meets the minimum requirements of American National Standard for Information Sciences—Permanence of Paper for Printed Library Materials, ANSI/NISO Z39.48-1992.

Contents

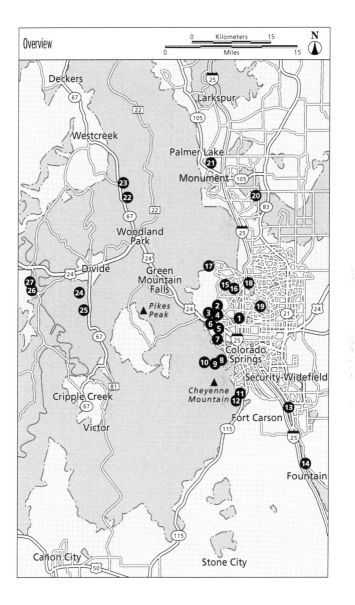

Kilometers

Miles

N

Deckers

Larkspur

Westcreek

Palmer Lake

Monument

Woodland Park

Green Mountain Falls

Divide

Pikes Peak

Colorado Springs

Security-Widefield

Cripple Creek

Cheyenne Mountain

Fort Carson

Victor

Cañon City

Stone City

Fountain

Map Legend

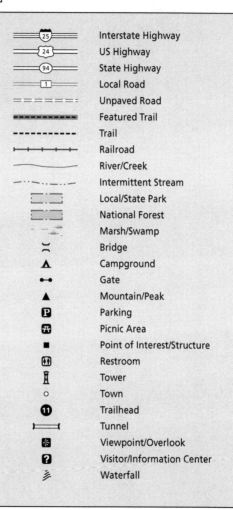

25	Interstate Highway
24	US Highway
94	State Highway
1	Local Road
	Unpaved Road
	Featured Trail
	Trail
	Railroad
	River/Creek
	Intermittent Stream
	Local/State Park
	National Forest
	Marsh/Swamp
	Bridge
	Campground
	Gate
	Mountain/Peak
	Parking
	Picnic Area
	Point of Interest/Structure
	Restroom
	Tower
	Town
11	Trailhead
	Tunnel
	Viewpoint/Overlook
	Visitor/Information Center
	Waterfall

Introduction

Colorado Springs is famed for its many recreational opportunities, beginning in the nineteenth century when visitors came for its mild climate and glorious natural wonders. The area has it all—long vistas of mountains, prairie, and sky; stunning attractions like Pikes Peak and Garden of the Gods; and over 1,000 miles of trails.

The greater Colorado Springs area offers excellent trails that thread through canyons, climb mountains, and traverse forests and grasslands. *Best Easy Day Hikes Colorado Springs* describes the best hikes and trails for the casual hiker within 35 miles of the city.

If you are on a tight schedule or want to do a short hike in a scenic area, the hikes in this book allow you to quickly select a day hike suited to your abilities and time constraints. Many of the hikes are between 1 and 3 miles long. Also included are nature walks for families and barrier-free trails that are wheelchair accessible. All the trailheads are easily reached by vehicle and have parking lots; some have facilities including water and restrooms. The hikes are rated by difficulty, being either easy or moderate. Check the Trail Finder to help you decide which hike is best for your party.

One of the best ways to enjoy, understand, and appreciate Colorado is by hiking its diverse terrain. Footpaths take you away from highways and roads and into ancient landscapes preserved in the rarified air, past ponds ringed with windswept grass, under shining mountains, and to the summits of high peaks with views that stretch forever. Every hiker interested in Colorado Springs' varied ecosystems, which range from desert and prairie to wet woodlands and the barren land above the trees, can learn much by hiking the region's many trails.

Best Easy Day Hikes Colorado Springs is about walking for pleasure—about the joy of putting on boots, shouldering a pack, and setting off into the world. Pick an easy trail and follow your feet. You'll find you can go just about anywhere.

Leave No Trace

Colorado Springs is an outdoors city. The U.S. Olympic Committee is headquartered in Colorado Springs. World-class runners and mountain bikers train on Colorado Springs' trails. One of the area's big sporting events is the Pikes Peak Marathon—26 miles and 8,000 vertical feet up and down America's most famous mountain. Called Olympic City USA, Colorado Springs is the longtime home of the U.S. Olympic & Paralympic Committee, the U.S. Olympic & Paralympic Training Center, more than two dozen National Governing Bodies and organizations, and the U.S. Olympic & Paralympic Museum and Hall of Fame.

The city boasts over 160 miles of park trails, 150 miles of urban trails, and over 9,000 acres of parkland. The beloved city park Garden of the Gods is recognized by TripAdvisor as the second best attraction in the United States and the ninth best in the world. Colorado Springs is simply a great place to get outside and enjoy wild nature.

With all the hikers in the Colorado Springs region, it's important to practice the Leave No Trace philosophy so that the area's natural resources and trails are protected from overuse and to maintain a positive experience for all visitors. Use the following Leave No Trace suggestions to make your own as well as everyone else's visit enjoyable and to protect our spectacular natural world.

Leave No Trace is about responsible outdoor ethics, including staying on the trail, not cutting switchbacks, packing out litter, keeping your dog leashed and picking up its waste, disposing properly of human waste, and leaving the environment as pristine as possible. Mountain and prairie ecosystems and environments are fragile and sensitive to human use. The marks of man, including social trails and damage from all-terrain vehicles and motorcycles, linger for years on this landscape.

Every hiker should adopt the Leave No Trace ethic to minimize his or her impact on this beautiful land. It's our responsibility to pay attention to our impact so that we can ensure that these trails will remain as wild refuges from the urban environment.

Always stay on the trail. Cutting switchbacks or traveling cross-country causes erosion and destroys plants. Always follow the route whenever possible. Steep slopes are susceptible to erosion caused by off-trail hiking.

Pack it in—pack it out. Everything you carry and use, including food wrappers, orange peels, cigarette butts, plastic bottles, and energy bar wrappers, needs to come out with you. Carry a plastic bag for picking up trash along the trail. Also, pick up your dog's waste and pack it out in a plastic bag. Too many dog owners leave their pet's feces in a plastic baggie on the trail.

Respect public and private property, livestock fences, and mining claims. Federal laws protect all archaeological and historic antiquities, including Native American artifacts, projectile points, ruins, petroglyphs, petrified wood, and historic sites. Don't carve your name on a rock surface or on a tree.

Before hiking, use the toilet at the trailhead, but if you require a bathroom break along the trail, be prepared with a kit that includes toilet paper or wet wipes. Double bag the kit in resealable plastic bags to keep the items fresh and dry. When you have to go, step off the trail to use them, bury all solid waste, and pack out all used items in an extra plastic bag. Many locations require that you pack out solid human waste as well, so use a WAG Bag, Restop, or other portable toilet kit, which are available at REI or Mountain Chalet in Colorado Springs. Dispose of the used kit in a proper location at the trailhead toilets or at home.

Take only photographs and memories. We can avoid leaving evidence of our passage across this delicate mountain environment. With care and sensitivity, we can all do our part to keep the Colorado Springs region beautiful, clean, and pristine. Leave natural features such as flowers or rocks where you found them. Enjoy their beauty but leave them for the next hiker. If everyone took one item, it wouldn't be long before nothing was left for others to enjoy.

For more information visit the Leave No Trace website at https://lnt.org.

Be Prepared

Hiking, although immensely rewarding, also comes with hazards and inherent risks, especially for those who come unprepared. Respect the mountain environment; be prepared and you'll be safe.

You must assume responsibility for your own actions and for your safety. Be aware of your surroundings and of potential dangers, including drop-offs, cliffs, and loose rock; the weather; and the physical condition of both your party and you. Never be afraid to turn around if conditions aren't right. Pay attention to those bad feelings—they keep you alive.

Here are a few suggestions to be prepared for emergency situations on your hike:

- Bring extra clothes and a raincoat, especially in the mountains. The weather can change in an instant. Heavy thunderstorms regularly occur on summer afternoons, and cold, wet clothing can lead to hypothermia.

- Colorado's Front Range has more lightning strikes than almost anywhere else in the United States. Pay attention to the weather and get off high places like ridges and summits before a storm arrives. If you can hear thunder, it's probably not safe to be outdoors.

- The air is thin and the sun is bright in the mountains. Summer temperatures can be hot. Wear a hat and use sunscreen to avoid sunburn.

- Carry plenty of water and sports drinks to replace electrolytes lost through sweating. Don't drink any water from streams unless you first treat and purify it.

- If you're coming from a lower elevation, watch for symptoms of altitude sickness, including headache, nausea, and loss of appetite. The best cure is to lose elevation.

- Allow enough time to complete your hike. If you start in the late afternoon, bring a headlamp or flashlight so that you can see the trail in the dark.

- Bring plenty of high-energy snacks for the trail and treats for the youngsters.

- Wear comfortable hiking shoes and good socks. Your feet will thank you. To avoid blisters, break in your shoes before wearing them in the backcountry.

- Enjoy the wildlife you see along the trail, but keep your distance and treat the animals with respect. Those cute little animals can bite and spread diseases like rabies.

Watchful mothers, including deer and black bears, are protective of their babies. Rattlesnakes are found on lower-elevation trails, so watch where you place your hands and feet. Don't feed wildlife to avoid disrupting their natural eating habits.

- Carry a day pack to tote all your trail needs, including rain gear, food, water, a first-aid kit, a flashlight, matches, and extra clothes. A whistle, GPS unit, topo map, binoculars, camera, pocketknife, and FalconGuide identification books for plants and animals are all handy additions. And don't forget your copy of *Best Easy Day Hikes Colorado Springs*!

Ranking the Hikes

The hikes in this book are either easy or moderate, depending on the length of the hike as well as the elevation gain. Here's a list of all the hikes ranging from easiest to most challenging.

Trail Finder

Best Hikes for Great Views

    Perkins Central Garden Trail

    Red Rock Canyon Loop

    Mount Cutler Trail

    Triple Treat, Rattlesnake Ridge, and Valley View Trails

    Grouse Mountain Overlook Trail

Best Hikes with Children

    Coyote Gulch Trail and Creek Bottom Trail Loop

    Fountain Creek Nature Trail

    Perkins Central Garden Trail

    Manitou Lake Trail

    Ponderosa Loop Trail

Best Hikes for Wildlife

    Fountain Creek Nature Trail

    Grouse Mountain Overlook Trail

    School Pond Trail

Best Hikes for Photographers

    Perkins Central Garden Trail

    Contemplative Trail to Sand Canyon Trail Loop

    Silver Cascade Falls and Buffalo Canyon Trails

    Grouse Mountain Overlook Trail

Best Hikes for Solitude

    Niobrara Trail to Ute Trail Connection Loop

Clear Spring Ranch Loop

Dry Creek, Red Squirrel, Wagon Wheel, and Wildflower Trails

Fallen Timbers Trail

School Pond Trail

Best Hikes for Rock Formations

Perkins Central Garden Trail

Siamese Twins Trail

Red Rock Canyon Loop

Contemplative Trail to Sand Canyon Trail Loop

Red Rocks Trail

1 Monument Valley Park: Monument Valley Park North Loop

This easy urban hike, following wide trails, explores the northern part of Monument Valley Park, a historic parkland north of downtown Colorado Springs.

Start: "Fontanero Street Trailhead"
Distance: 1.1 miles
Hiking time: About 1 hour
Type of hike: Loop
Trail names: Monument Valley Park Loop, Pikes Peak Greenway Trail
Difficulty: Easy. Cumulative elevation gain is 40 feet.
Trail surface: Double-track dirt trail
Best season: Year-round
Other trail users: Bicyclists
Restrictions: Park hours are 5 a.m. to 10 p.m. May through Oct, 5 a.m. to 9 p.m. Nov through Apr. Leashed dogs allowed; pet waste must be picked up and disposed of by the pet owner. Stay on designated trails. Park in designated areas and parking lots. Motorized vehicles prohibited. No littering, alcoholic beverages, smoking, camping, dumping, tree cutting, or fires.
Maps: Colorado Springs Parks, Recreation and Cultural Services website; USGS Colorado Springs
Trail contact: Colorado Springs Parks, Recreation and Cultural Services, (719) 385-5940

Finding the trailhead: From I-25, take exit 143 and drive east on Uintah Street for 0.5 mile to North Cascade Avenue. Turn left onto North Cascade and drive north for 0.7 mile to West Fontanero Street. Turn left on West Fontanero Street and drive west for 0.2 mile, and park on the right in a long strip lot where Fontanero bends left and becomes Culebra Avenue. The informally named "Fontanero Street Trailhead" is on the west side of the lot at a gap in a wood rail fence. Street address: 205 West Fontanero Street. GPS: 38.860666, -104.828565

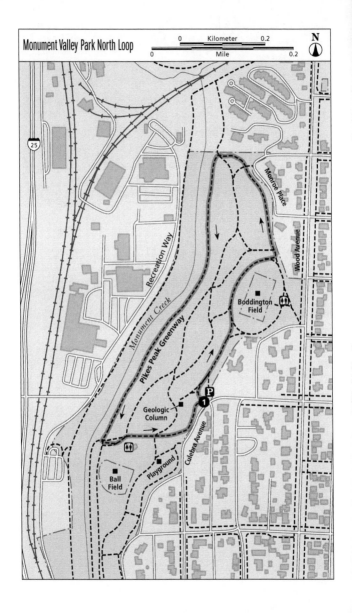

The Hike

The Monument Valley Park North Loop hike makes an easy counterclockwise loop around the northern end of 153-acre Monument Valley Park, which stretches alongside Monument Creek north of downtown Colorado Springs. Following wide, easy trails, this book's only urban hike offers local history, recreation sites, and wonderful views west of Pikes Peak. Besides walkers, the park's trails are busy with bicyclists and runners.

Monument Valley Park, listed on the National Register of Historic Places in 2007, preserves the rich heritage of Colorado Springs. Like other iconic city parklands, including Palmer Park and North Cheyenne Cañon, Monument Valley Park was given to the city by General William Jackson Palmer, the 1871 founder of Colorado Springs, in 1907. Where cattle once grazed, Palmer hired engineer Edmond van Diest and landscape architect Charles W. Leavitt Jr. to design formal gardens, winding footpaths, bridges, and ponds and plant at least one tree of every Colorado species.

Later, the park was reimagined after a disastrous flood on Memorial Day 1935 erased much of the park's structures, including bridges, trails, and a lake. In the late 1930s, the Works Progress Administration (WPA) rechanneled the creek, lined its banks with rock, repaired flood damage, and built features like benches, walls, and stairs with native stone.

The hike begins at the "Fontanero Street Trailhead" and heads north on a wide trail, passing Boddington Field, a soccer pitch that was formerly a reservoir to store irrigation water and fed a waterfall at the Geologic Column. Past the field, the trail bends west beneath towering cottonwood trees and follows the Pikes Peak Greenway Trail south above the east bank of Monument Creek. After crossing a stone bridge, the hike turns left and follows a closed service road past a baseball field and up a hill to the trailhead.

Other unnamed trails thread through cottonwoods east of the Greenway, offering more quiet hikes. The Pikes Peak Greenway Trail continues south from the hike to downtown Colorado Springs. The Greenway Trail, part of the Front Range Trail, runs almost 17 miles through Colorado Springs from south of the Air Force Academy to Fountain.

Miles and Directions

0.0 Start at the "Fontanero Street Trailhead" on the west side of the parking strip and walk west 40 feet to a junction. Go right and hike north on the wide trail atop a bluff.

0.1 Reach a Y junction at the southwest corner of Boddington Field (GPS: 38.861951, -104.827912), a soccer pitch. Keep left and walk north along the west side of the field. At its north end, the trail bends right.

0.25 Reach a junction at the field's north side and go left on a wide trail. Walk north below tall cottonwoods on the park's east boundary and then bend west.

0.45 Reach a junction with the Pikes Peak Greenway Trail (GPS: 38.865771,-104.828146) and go left on it. Hike south above a sloping stone wall built in the 1930s to channel Monument Creek. Enjoy spacious views west of Pikes Peak and the sound of rushing water on three rapids in the creek below.

0.9 Cross an old bridge over a park service road and reach a junction (GPS: 38.859755, -104.831373). Go left (east) on the closed road/trail and pass restrooms (summer only), a ball field, and a playground on the right. For an interesting side trek, visit the Geologic Column on the left (see option).

If not, hike up a steep hill and bend left alongside Culebra Avenue to return to the trailhead.

1.1 Arrive back at the trailhead (GPS: 38.860666, -104.828565).

Option: At the base of the hill, take the trail on the left and walk north 300 feet to the base of the semicircular Geologic Column, a park historic site. The column depicts a billion years of geologic history of the Pikes Peak region in ten distinct layers, ranging from Pikes Peak granite at the base to Lyons sandstone from Garden of the Gods, and topped with Niobrara sandstone from Austin Bluffs. A 19-foot waterfall, fed by a ditch from today's Boddington Field, poured off the right side of the column until 1956. General Palmer commissioned the unique exhibit for the park's opening in 1907. After viewing the site, return south to the trail and go left.

2 Garden of the Gods: Gateway Trail to Perkins Central Garden Trail Loop

This classic hike follows a paved trail through the major rock formations in Garden of the Gods, including North Gateway Rock, South Gateway Rock, Grey Rock, and Montezuma's Tower.

Start: Parking Lot 1 trailhead
Distance: 2.25 miles
Hiking time: About 1 hour
Type of hike: Lollipop loop
Trail names: Gateway Trail, Perkins Central Garden Trail, Upper Loop Trail (option)
Difficulty: Easy. Wheelchair accessible. Cumulative elevation gain is 170 feet; gain including Upper Loop Trail is 224 feet.
Trail surface: Concrete trail
Best season: Mar through Nov
Other trail users: Hikers only
Restrictions: Park hours are 5 a.m. to 9 p.m. Nov through Apr, 5 a.m. to 10 p.m. May through Oct.

Leashed dogs allowed; pet waste must be picked up by the pet owner. No bicycles. Stay on designated trails. Park in designated parking lots. No littering, alcoholic beverages, smoking, camping, dumping, tree cutting, or fires.
Maps: Colorado Springs Parks, Recreation and Cultural Services website; USGS Manitou Springs
Trail contacts: Colorado Springs Parks, Recreation and Cultural Services, (719) 385-5940; Garden of the Gods Visitor & Nature Center, (719) 634-6666 or (719) 219-0108

Finding the trailhead: From I-25, take Garden of the Gods Road exit 146 and drive west for 2.4 miles until it dead-ends at North 30th Street. Go left on North 30th and drive south for 1.5 miles to a roundabout. Take the first right and drive into Garden of the Gods on Gateway Road. Take an immediate left into the large Parking Lot 1. The

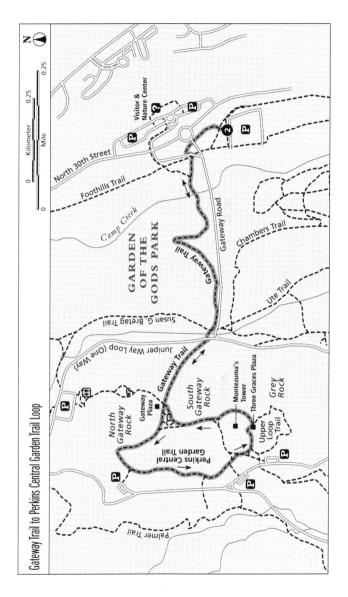

Gateway Trail to Perkins Central Garden Trail Loop

trailhead is on the northeast side of the parking lot. GPS: 38.876691, -104.870636

The Hike

This spectacular hike follows the Gateway Trail to the Perkins Central Garden Trail, a paved path that loops through the central Garden zone and explores Garden of the Gods' soaring sandstone formations. Beginning at Parking Lot 1 on the east side of the park, the paved, wheelchair-accessible hike offers scenic views, gentle grades, and interpretive signs. This hike is simply one that every Colorado Springs resident and visitor should enjoy.

Garden of the Gods, nestled against the Rampart Range on the west side of Colorado Springs, is an outdoor sculpture garden dominated by rock monuments. Here rise uplifted layers of sandstone that tell the geologic story of the changing earth—the uplift and erosion of mountains, periodic inundations of seas, and the coming and going of ancient lives. The story of the earth from a couple billion years ago until the present is at Garden of the Gods. Few other places in the United States boast the variety and age of exposed rock found here.

The hike begins at the northeast corner of Parking Lot 1 on the east side of Garden of the Gods near the visitor center and 30th Street. While the Perkins Trail can also be accessed from Parking Lot 2, it is better to start at Lot 1 since it has more available parking, especially in the summer months.

The first hike segment follows the paved Gateway Trail west from the parking lot and trailhead to its junction with the Juniper Way Loop, a one-way road that loops around the main Garden area. After crossing the road, the trail continues west to Gateway Plaza in an open gap between North and South Gateway Rocks. The Gateway Trail ends at its junction with the connector trail from Parking Lot 1 to the north.

Stop at Gateway Plaza to admire the sandstone cliffs and formations, including North Gateway Rock, also called Gate Rock, on the right. This huge formation, the highest in the Garden, looms 300 feet above the plaza. South Gateway Rock rises sheer above the south side of the plaza. Sit on a wall in the Gateway to enjoy the views or watch rock climbers scale the ruddy walls.

A metal plaque on the south face of North Gateway Rock details the gift of Garden of the Gods to Colorado Springs and honors its benefactor, railroad magnate Charles Elliott Perkins. Perkins purchased the area in 1879 but allowed public visitation. Two years after his death in 1907, his children donated the land as a park that would "be kept forever open and free to the public."

The Perkins Central Garden Trail begins at the Gateway, forming a loop through the rock formations. Take the right fork and hike beneath the west face of North Gateway Rock to an overlook with interpretive signs. The trail heads south along a meadow's edge with great views of the Gateway Rocks. Continue to Three Graces Plaza at the paved trail's southern end. Looming above the circular plaza is 135-foot-high Montezuma's Tower on the right and the narrow fins of the Three Graces.

Hike east from the plaza. (*Option:* As you descend, look right for the Upper Loop Trail, a marked dirt trail. Take this to add a scenic 0.2-mile loop to the hike. The trail climbs south to a rocky overlook north of Keyhole Rock. Descend back to the paved trail by continuing west on it until it meets the Perkins Trail west of Three Graces Plaza.)

Continue north on the Perkins Trail with South Gateway Rock's west face rising beyond a wooden fence. From the earliest days, the Garden's bizarre rocks have teased the imaginations of visitors who saw fanciful shapes, some reflected by names like Weeping Indian and Kissing Camels. Kissing Camels is a skyline arch perched atop North Gateway. The Weeping Indian is a profile of white rock that faces north on the west face of South Gateway Rock.

Continue north along the trail, bending east to Gateway Plaza, and then retrace your steps east on Gateway Trail to the trailhead.

Miles and Directions

0.0 From the trailhead on the northeast side of the parking lot, hike 125 feet on a paved trail to a junction with the Foothills Trail and follow it through a tunnel beneath Gateway Road.

0.1 Reach a junction on the left with the Gateway Trail. Go left on the paved trail and hike west across Camp Creek, up a hillside, and parallel to Gateway Road.

0.6 Reach the Juniper Way Loop (GPS: 38.877203, -104.877921) and cross the road at a marked crosswalk. Continue west on the paved Gateway Trail to Gateway Plaza in a gap with North Gateway Rock on the right and South Gateway Rock on the left.

0.75 At the east side of the Gateway, reach the end of the Gateway Trail and a junction on the right with a paved trail that goes north to Parking Lot 2 (GPS: 38.878442, -104.880318). Keep right on the paved Perkins Central Garden Trail (left of the metal plaque) to make a counterclockwise loop through the central Garden area. Hike northwest beneath the West Face of North Gateway Rock. Look up to see the Kissing Camels, a small arch perched on North Gateway's skyline ridge. Farther north, stop at an overlook with park info and then go left on the trail.

0.9 Meet a junction with a short trail that goes right to Parking Lot 4, the wheelchair-accessible lot. Continue south on the Perkins Trail along a meadow's west edge. The meadow is fenced and off-limits to hiking to protect the grassland and wildlife.

1.15 Reach a trail junction on the left with a paved connector trail that goes east for 0.1 mile and rejoins the Perkins Trail. (*Option:* To shorten the hike, take this cutoff.) Continue southeast on the paved trail.

1.2 Reach Three Graces Plaza (GPS: 38.875935, -104.881305), an overlook below two finlike spires—Montezuma's Tower and Three Graces—at the loop's south end. Continue east (*option:* go right on the Upper Loop Trail for a scenic 0.2-mile side loop) and then north on the paved trail, passing below South Gateway Rock and keeping right to return to Gateway Plaza.

1.5 Reach the junction with the Gateway Trail at the east side of the Gateway and go right on it. Hike east to the crosswalk at the Juniper Way Loop and continue back to Parking Lot 1.

2.25 Arrive back at the trailhead (GPS: 38.876691, -104.870636).

3 Garden of the Gods: Siamese Twins Trail

This lovely trail leads you through shallow canyons in Garden of the Gods to a scenic vista amid sandstone pillars.

Start: Informal trailhead at Parking Lot 16
Distance: 0.55 mile
Hiking time: 30 minutes to 1 hour
Type of hike: Loop
Trail name: Siamese Twins Trail
Difficulty: Easy. Cumulative elevation gain is 108 feet.
Trail surface: Single-track dirt trail
Best season: Mar through Nov; trails may be icy or muddy in winter.
Other trail users: Equestrians
Restrictions: Park hours are 5 a.m. to 9 p.m. Nov through Apr, 5 a.m. to 10 p.m. May through Oct. Park gates locked at closing time.

Leashed dogs allowed; pet waste must be picked up by the pet owner. No bicycles. Stay on designated trails. Park in designated parking lots. No littering, alcoholic beverages, smoking, camping, dumping, tree cutting, or fires.
Maps: Colorado Springs Parks, Recreation and Cultural Services website; USGS Manitou Springs
Trail contacts: Colorado Springs Parks, Recreation and Cultural Services, (719) 385-5940; Garden of the Gods Visitor & Nature Center, (719) 634-6666 or (719) 219-0108

Finding the trailhead: Take the Cimarron (US 24 West) exit from I-25 and drive west for 2.6 miles. Turn right onto 31st Street and then left onto Colorado Avenue after 1 block. Drive west on Colorado to a right turn on Beckers Lane, which leads to Garden of the Gods Trading Post. Here you veer right onto Garden Lane. Take the first left to continue on Garden Drive. Turn right into the Spring Canyon trailhead parking lot. The trail begins in the northwest corner of the

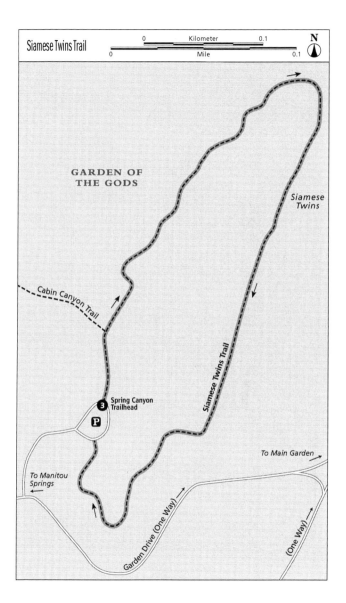

Siamese Twins Trail

0   Kilometer   0.1

0   Mile   0.1

N

GARDEN OF
THE GODS

Siamese
Twins

Cabin Canyon Trail

Siamese Twins Trail

3 Spring Canyon
Trailhead

P

To Main Garden

To Manitou
Springs

Garden Drive (One Way)

(One Way)

lot, where you will also find a map of area trails. GPS: 38.868234, -104.890359

The Hike

Garden of the Gods, the most famous natural wonder near Colorado Springs, needs to be at the top of every hiker's must-see list. A variety of hiking trails explore this spectacular city park. The Siamese Twins Trail, one of the area's less-traveled easy hikes, offers an excellent opportunity to get off the beaten path in the southwest sector of the park.

The hike begins at a marked trailhead at the northwest corner of the parking lot. Walk north along a split-rail fence, passing the Cabin Canyon Trail junction on the left. Stay right, following a trail marker and climbing occasional steps.

The trail follows a sandstone arroyo through a pygmy forest of scrub oak, piñon pine, and juniper. The Fountain Formation sandstone, a thick layer of sedimentary rock tilted up against the mountains, was deposited along the eastern edge of the Ancestral Rocky Mountains about 300 million years ago. Notice its coarse composition of pebbles and cobbles, which were washed off the mountains and deposited in broad alluvial fans along the edge of an ancient sea.

A second set of stairs leads to a dry streambed, which you ford by a dirt bridge built on a culvert. As the trail continues, sandstone formations appear above spiny yucca and twisted juniper trees. The trail circles southeast toward the Siamese Twins, two conjoined pinnacles. Clamber up left behind the spires at a trail marker at 0.3 mile to a marvelous view point. To the south rise the sandstone humps of Red Rock Canyon, with Cheyenne Mountain and the Front Range looming in the distance. You will find an interesting and unique view of Pikes Peak through an eroded window at the base of the Siamese Twins, providing a wonderful photo opportunity in morning light.

To descend back to the trailhead and parking lot, circle around to the west side of the Twins, then rejoin the trail at a marker and go left (south). Pass a second trail marker at the base of a great slab of red rock, and hike beside a log fence. The winding path takes you down the spine of a ridge, then along a second log fence to another trail marker. Turn right (west) here. The park road is visible to your left. From here it's a quick hop (0.25 mile) down some stairs to the parking lot.

Miles and Directions

0.0 Begin at the trailhead on the north side of the parking lot (GPS: 38.868234, -104.890359). Walk the trail clockwise.

0.3 Reach the Siamese Twins (GPS: 38.869957, -104.888472).

0.55 Arrive back at the trailhead on the south side of the parking lot (GPS: 38.867935, -104.890476).

4 Garden of the Gods: Niobrara Trail to Ute Trail Connection Loop

Following a hogback on the Niobrara Trail, this hike offers superb views of Pikes Peak and Garden of the Gods before descending and returning to the trailhead on the Ute Trail Connection.

Start: Trailhead at south end of South Garden Parking Lot
Distance: 1.3 miles
Hiking time: About 1 hour
Type of hike: Loop
Trail names: Ute Trail, Niobrara Trail, Ute Trail Connection
Difficulty: Easy. Cumulative elevation gain is 189 feet.
Trail surface: Dirt trail
Best season: Mar through Nov; trails may be muddy in winter.
Other trail users: Mountain bikers
Restrictions: Park hours are 5 a.m. to 9 p.m. Nov through Apr, 5 a.m. to 10 p.m. May through Oct. Leashed dogs allowed; pet waste must be picked up by the pet owner. Stay on designated trails. Park in designated parking lots. No littering, alcoholic beverages, smoking, camping, dumping, tree cutting, or fires.
Maps: Colorado Springs Parks, Recreation and Cultural Services website; USGS Manitou Springs
Trail contacts: Colorado Springs Parks, Recreation and Cultural Services, (719) 385-5940; Garden of the Gods Visitor & Nature Center, (719) 634-6666 or (719) 219-0108

Finding the trailhead: From I-25, take Garden of the Gods Road exit 146 and drive west for 2.4 miles until it dead-ends at North 30th Street. Go left on North 30th and drive south for 1.5 miles to a roundabout. Take the first right and drive into Garden of the Gods on Gateway Road. Drive 0.4 mile to one-way Juniper Way Loop and go

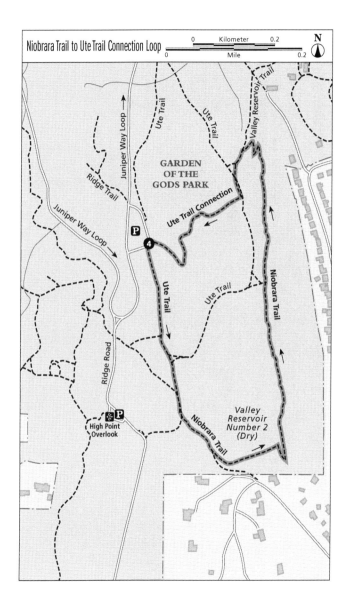

0   Kilometer   0.2

0   Mile   0.2

N

Ute Trail

Juniper Way Loop

Valley Reservoir Trail

Ute Trail

Ridge Trail

GARDEN
OF THE
GODS PARK

Ute Trail Connection

Juniper Way Loop

P

4

Ute Trail

Ute Trail

Niobrara Trail

Ridge Road

P

High Point
Overlook

Niobrara Trail

Valley
Reservoir
Number 2
(Dry)

right. Follow it for 1.8 miles and turn right into the South Garden Parking Lot (P10). The trailhead is on the parking lot's south side. GPS: 38.869243, -104.878037

The Hike

Following three trails, this hike forms a loop in the southeast corner of Garden of the Gods. The easy-to-follow trails are both double and single track with a solid footbed, occasional rocky sections, markers at trail junctions, and minimal elevation gain. Unlike most Garden hikes, these trails see low use, so you seldom encounter other hikers, especially in the morning and evening. This area of the park is open to mountain biking, but it is rare to meet a biker. Besides fun walking and solitude, the hike offers spectacular views west of 14,109-foot Pikes Peak and northwest to the sandstone formations in the main Garden zone.

Start the hike at the South Garden Parking Lot (P10), a large parking area on the east side of Juniper Way Loop, a one-way road that loops around Garden of the Gods. From a trailhead at the south end of the lot, walk past a metal gate and head south on the Ute Trail, which begins as a dirt service road. Past a park maintenance area, follow the Niobrara Trail, which heads southeast and crosses the top of an earthen levee built for flood control, and climb to the crest of Niobrara Ridge.

This long north-to-south ridge forms a hogback on the park's eastern edge. The trail twists along the ridgeline, passing buff-colored cliffs composed of the Niobrara Formation. The formation, a mix of limestone and shale, was deposited between 70 and 88 million years ago in the Cretaceous Seaway, a shallow strait that covered most of Colorado at the end of the dinosaur era. Look for marine fossils in the bedrock, including imprints of clams and ammonites.

At the ridge's north end, the trail drops down to the Valley Reservoir Trail. Finish the hike by turning left and hiking up the Ute Trail, then heading right on the Ute Trail Connection, which climbs over a hill and descends to a trailhead on the southeast side of the parking lot.

Miles and Directions

0.0 From the trailhead (GPS: 38.869243, -104.878037), go past a gate and hike south on a dirt service road (Ute Trail).

0.2 After passing a junction and dirt service area on the right, reach a junction on the left with the Ute Trail (GPS: 38.866966, -104.877412). Continue straight (right) onto the Niobrara Trail and hike south.

0.25 Reach a Y junction with a trail that goes right to Ridge Road (GPS: 38.866133, -104.877153). Continue straight on the Niobrara Trail and bend left (east) and cross the top of a flood levee north of houses. Climb the west side of Niobrara Ridge.

0.5 Reach the ridgetop (GPS: 38.864664, -104.874033) and go left on the Niobrara Trail. Hike north along the ridge, passing view points of Pikes Peak to the west and the Garden's rocks to the northwest.

0.75 Dip to a saddle and a junction with two connector trails that go left to the Ute Trail (GPS: 38.868509, -104.874659). Continue straight on the Niobrara Trail and hike north on the ridgeline. At its north end, descend the trail.

1.0 Reach a junction with the Chambers Trail / Valley Reservoir Trail (GPS: 38.871352, -104.875339) and go left. Hike past a junction on the left to the Ute Trail and reach a junction with the Ute Trail. Keep straight on it and hike up a slight hill.

1.1 Reach a junction on the right with the Ute Trail Connection (GPS: 38.870363, -104.875347) and go right on it. Hike to a ridge and drop down its west side, passing a right turn to an overlook.

1.3 Arrive at a trailhead on the southeast side of the parking lot (GPS: 38.869396, -104.877919) that is 60 feet from the starting trailhead.

5 Red Rock Canyon Open Space: Red Rock Canyon Loop

Explore Red Rock Canyon's timeless beauty by hiking into the canyon's scenic sandstone heart, passing soaring cliffs, grazing mule deer, and the remnants of the historic Kenmuir Quarry.

Start: Red Rock Canyon Trailhead

Distance: 2.15 miles

Hiking time: 1 to 2 hours

Type of hike: Lollipop loop

Trail names: Red Rock Canyon Trail, Quarry Pass Trail, Red Rock Canyon Path

Difficulty: Easy. Cumulative elevation gain is 316 feet.

Trail surface: Double-track and single-track dirt trail

Best season: Mar through Nov; trails may be icy, snowpacked, or muddy in winter.

Other trail users: Mountain bikers, equestrians

Restrictions: Park hours are 5 a.m. to 9 p.m. Nov through Apr, 5 a.m. to 10 p.m. May through Oct. Leashed dogs allowed; pet waste must be picked up by the pet owner. Stay on designated trails. Park in designated parking lots. No littering, alcoholic beverages, smoking, camping, dumping, tree cutting, or fires. No rock scrambling or rock climbing without an annual climbing permit and proper climbing equipment.

Maps: Colorado Springs Parks, Recreation and Cultural Services website; USGS Manitou Springs

Trail contact: Colorado Springs Parks, Recreation and Cultural Services, (719) 385-5940

Finding the trailhead: Red Rock Canyon Open Space is south of US 24 on the west side of Colorado Springs. From downtown Colorado Springs and I-25, take the Cimarron Street / US 24 exit (exit 141) and drive west for 3.1 miles. From the left turn lane on US 24,

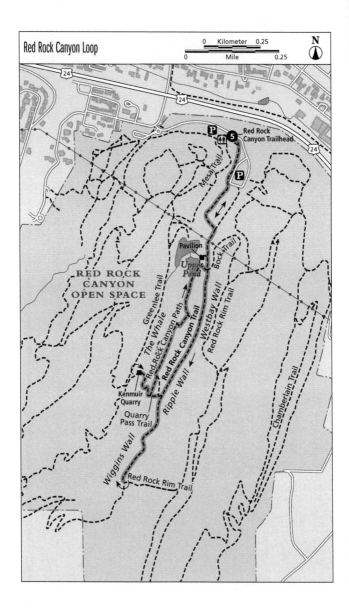

turn left (south) onto South Ridge Road, which is the only left turn between 31st Street and the first Manitou Springs exit. Use extreme caution turning on and off the busy highway. Drive south on South Ridge Road for 0.1 mile and turn left into the park. Drive through a roundabout and take the second right turn. Drive east for 0.1 mile and turn right into a large parking lot. The Red Rock Canyon Trailhead is at the east end of the parking lot. GPS: 38.853335, -104.879191

For an alternative parking lot, continue east on the road past the turnoff into the main lot and drive 0.3 mile to a parking lot and trailhead at the north end of Red Rock Canyon. GPS: 38.851354, -104.878473

The Hike

This hike explores Red Rock Canyon, the captivating centerpiece of the 1,474-acre Red Rock Canyon Open Space. In 2003 the city of Colorado Springs purchased the park's initial 787 acres, saving the area from trophy homes, a golf course, and resort development. Stretching south from the trailhead, salmon-colored sandstone cliffs, Gambel oak groves, cottonwood trees, grassy meadows, and a relic stand of quaking aspens fill scenic Red Rock Canyon. Besides its natural beauty and dramatic geological formations, the canyon harbors archaeological and historical sites, including the Kenmuir stone quarry that operated from 1886 through 1915.

The hike begins at the Red Rock Canyon Trailhead on the east side of the main parking lot. Portable toilets and a trail map are at the trailhead. An alternative parking area is located past the first parking area at the end of the park road below Red Rock Canyon. If you park here, knock 0.2 mile off your round-trip hike distance.

The first trail segment runs along the left side of a freeride bike area and then bends south and passes the south parking lot and a ruddy cliff quarried in the nineteenth century. The trail gently climbs and joins a closed road. (If you started from the south parking lot, it's 0.1 mile to this point.)

The next leg heads south on the Red Rock Canyon Trail, passing the site of the old Bock house, now a shady pavilion. Red Rock Canyon once belonged to John George Bock, who built the house in the 1920s. He started with a tourist camp and stables and then acquired land from stone companies and for back taxes. After Bock's death, his two sons, John and Richard, wanted to develop a World Trade Center here with homes, office buildings, a sports arena, and thirteen lakes. They were unable to get the area zoned for the project, so in the 1970s part of the area became a landfill and gravel pit. In the 1990s another developer attempted to resurrect the Bock plan but was denied annexation by both Manitou Springs and Colorado Springs, leaving the door open for its purchase as parkland in 2003.

The trail continues up the canyon's east side, passing popular cliffs for climbing, and finishes at a turnaround point west of Don Ellis Point, the high point of the hogback on the eastern skyline. From the turnaround, retrace your steps north to the Quarry Pass Trail and go left, climbing to Quarry Pass in the historic Kenmuir Quarry. In the nineteenth century, sandstone blocks quarried here were loaded onto train cars on a railroad spur that ran into the canyon and then shipped to Denver, Kansas, and Texas. The stone, however, didn't weather well, and the canyon's quarries closed by 1915.

After visiting the quarry, return to the canyon and take the first left on the Red Rock Canyon Path. Follow this north past Solar Slab, a popular climbing cliff, and the upper pond to the pavilion. Return to the trailhead on the Red Rock Canyon Trail.

Miles and Directions

0.0 Begin at the Red Rock Canyon Trailhead at the east end of the main parking lot. Hike east and south past the free-ride area into the mouth of Red Rock Canyon.

0.1 Reach a trail that goes left to the south parking lot adjacent to the trail. Continue south past a picnic area on the left and ascend a hill.

0.3 Reach a junction with a closed service road (GPS: 38.849714, -104.879662) and go right on the road. Hike south past a gate.

0.35 Reach a pavilion, interpretive signs about Red Rock Canyon's history, and the upper pond. Continue south on the Red Rock Canyon Trail.

0.4 Reach a junction on the right with the Red Rock Canyon Path (GPS: 38.848179, -104.880064). Continue south on the trail, passing below cliffs, including Westbay Wall, Sayers Wall, and Ripple Wall, on the east side of the canyon.

0.75 Meet a junction on the right with the Quarry Pass Trail (GPS: 38.843289, -104.882430). You will follow it to the quarry on your return hike. Continue south on the trail and climb a hill.

1.0 Arrive at a junction atop the hill with the Red Rock Rim Trail on the left (GPS: 38.839944, -104.884450). This is the turnaround point for the hike and the end of the Red Rock Canyon Trail, which continues south as the Roundup Trail. After enjoying the canyon, retrace the trail north.

1.25 Reach the junction with the Quarry Pass Trail. Go left on the trail and hike west across a meadow.

1.3 Reach a junction on the right with the Red Rock Canyon Path. You will return to this junction on the return hike. Continue west and climb the rocky trail. Below the quarry, you can climb a stone staircase carved in the 1880s or go left on an easier trail.

1.4 Arrive at the historic Kenmuir Quarry (GPS: 38.844148, -104.883449). After visiting the quarry, hike back down the trail.

1.5 Reach the junction with the Red Rock Canyon Path (GPS: 38.843320, -104.883033) and go left on the single-track trail. Hike north on the west side of the canyon, passing beneath The Whale and Solar Slab, both popular climbing cliffs.

1.75 Reach a junction with a connector trail to the Red Rock Canyon Trail on the right. Continue north on the Red Rock Canyon Path, following the west edge of a meadow to the upper pond. This scenic pond is unfortunately drying up since the park isn't replenishing its water. Go right and meet the Red Rock Canyon Trail south of the pavilion. Go left on it to finish the hike.

2.15 Arrive back at the trailhead (GPS: 38.853335, -104.879191).

6 Red Rock Canyon Open Space: Contemplative Trail to Sand Canyon Trail Loop

This excellent hike threads through soaring sandstone fins and thickets of Gambel oak on a hikers-only trail on the west side of Red Rock Canyon Open Space.

Start: Sand Canyon Trailhead

Distance: 1.65 miles

Hiking time: 1 to 2 hours

Type of hike: Lollipop loop

Trail names: Contemplative Trail, Sand Canyon Trail

Difficulty: Easy. Cumulative elevation gain is 215 feet.

Trail surface: Dirt trail

Best season: Mar through Nov; trails may be icy or muddy in winter.

Other trail users: Mountain bikers; hikers only on Contemplative Trail

Restrictions: Park hours are 5 a.m. to 9 p.m. Nov through Apr, 5 a.m. to 10 p.m. May through Oct. Leashed dogs allowed; pet waste must be picked up by the pet owner. Stay on designated trails. Park in designated parking lots. No littering, alcoholic beverages, smoking, camping, dumping, tree cutting, or fires. No e-bikes or other motorized devices, including power scooters, hoverboards, electric skateboards, ATVs, motorcycles, and remote-control vehicles.

Maps: Colorado Springs Parks, Recreation and Cultural Services website; USGS Manitou Springs

Trail contact: Colorado Springs Parks, Recreation and Cultural Services, (719) 385-5940

Finding the trailhead: Red Rock Canyon Open Space is south of Garden of the Gods and US 24 on the west side of Colorado Springs. From downtown Colorado Springs and I-25, take the Cimarron Street/

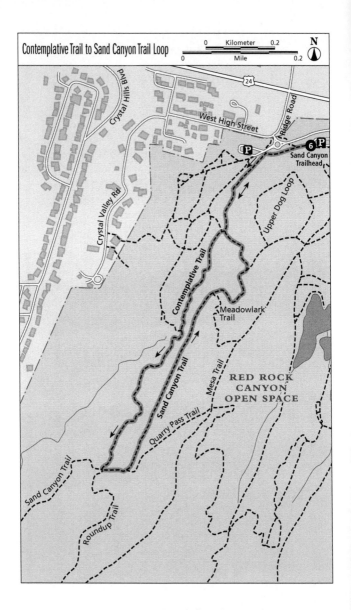

US 24 exit (exit 141) and drive west for 3.1 miles. From the left turn lane on US 24, turn left (south) onto South Ridge Road, which is the only left turn between 31st Street and the first Manitou Springs exit. Use extreme caution turning on and off the busy highway. Drive south on Ridge Road for 0.1 mile and turn left into the park. Drive through a roundabout and take the second right turn. Drive east for 0.1 mile and turn right into a large parking lot. The Sand Canyon Trailhead is at the west end of the lot. GPS: 38.853534, -104.881429

The Hike

The Contemplative Trail and Sand Canyon Trail form a wonderful hike at Red Rock Canyon Open Space. The hike wanders through uptilted fins of sandstone, dense thickets of Gambel oak, scattered ponderosa pines, and meadows strewn with summer wildflowers. Open only to hikers, the Contemplative Trail offers several benches to listen to birdsong and admire mountain views. Watch for wildlife in the broad valley below the trail, including mule deer, coyotes, black bears, and red-tailed hawks wheeling across the sky. The return hike follows the Sand Canyon Trail, paralleling the same rock formations on their east side.

The hike begins at the Sand Canyon Trailhead on the parking lot's west side. Portable toilets sit at the lot's east end. Hike southwest and join the Sand Canyon Trail below Bock Fin, a soaring cliff composed of 300-million-year-old Fountain Formation sandstone. This coarse rock, filled with gravel and cobbles, was deposited on the east flank of the Ancestral Rocky Mountains, forming a thick layer that was later tilted upward when today's Rockies rose.

After a quarter mile, the hike joins the Contemplative Trail, originally named Garden of the Goddesses Trail, and heads south beneath tall rock formations, dipping through shallow vales and climbing short hills. One spectacular section squeezes through a rock-walled passageway. The trail ends at the Sand Canyon Trail.

Turn left here and follow the Sand Canyon Trail north past junctions with the Quarry Pass and Meadowlark Trails and a series of tilted stone slabs dubbed the Ironing Boards. Finish by keeping left on the Sand Canyon Trail at its junction with the Upper Dog Loop Trail and returning north on the Contemplative Trail.

Miles and Directions

0.0 Start at the Sand Canyon Trailhead. Pass signs with regulations, a park map, and interpretive info. Hike west on the Sand Canyon Trail alongside the park road and a roundabout.

0.1 Reach a junction with an alternative parking lot to the right. Keep left on the Sand Canyon Trail, pass another junction with a trail from the parking lot, and bend left. Hike southwest on the wide trail.

0.25 Reach a junction and go left on the Contemplative Trail (GPS: 38.852536, -104.884242). Hike southeast to the base of Bock Fin, a soaring wall named for John Bock, the previous owner of Red Rock Canyon. Hike south on the peaceful trail, dipping across a shallow canyon to a junction with the return trail on the left. Continue south, climbing steps and passing below the west cliff of another fin. A bench below a pine gives views west of Pikes Peak. Descend a hill and then climb stone steps.

0.4 Reach a junction with the main trail going left to the base of a fin. For excitement, take the right trail and hike through a rock-walled corridor. At its end, step left and return to the main trail. Descend a staircase of thirty-nine timber steps to another gap between fins.

0.5 Reach a four-way junction with the Sand Canyon Trail in the gap (GPS: 38.848603, -104.886001). Keep right on the Contemplative Trail and climb timber steps to the north end of Gaia Tower, the tallest sandstone fin. Pass below its vertical cliff and climb a slope through oaks.

0.6 Meet a junction on the left (GPS: 38.847628,-104.887242) with a short trail that climbs steps and goes left to an overlook. Return to the main trail and continue south, passing beside cliffs and below shady pines and Gambel oak thickets. Past the last formation, climb timber steps.

0.8 Reach the end of the Contemplative Trail and a four-way junction with the Sand Canyon Trail crossing left to right and the Roundup Trail straight ahead (GPS: 38.845267,-104.888593). Go left on the Sand Canyon Trail for the return loop.

0.85 Reach a junction on the right with the Quarry Pass Trail. Continue along the main trail, bending left and hiking north. The trail passes the Ironing Boards, a row of tilted sandstone fins with smooth faces, and gently descends past the steep east face of Gaia Tower.

1.1 Reach a junction with a spur of the Sand Canyon Trail that goes left, passes the Contemplative Trail, and continues into Sand Canyon. Continue straight on the Sand Canyon Trail and then bend away from the rocks and hike through a couple wide bends to a junction with the Upper Dog Loop Trail (GPS: 38.850395, -104.883629). Go left on the Sand Canyon Trail and descend northwest down slopes and steps.

1.4 Reach a junction with the Contemplative Trail in a clearing (GPS: 38.851346, -104.884399). Go right on the Contemplative Trail, climbing to the west base of Bock Fin and then dropping northwest.

1.5 Return to the start of the Contemplative Trail at its junction with the Sand Canyon Trail (GPS: 38.852536, -104.884242). Go right and hike northwest past the parking lot on the left.

1.65 Arrive back at the trailhead (GPS: 38.853534, -104.881429).

7 Bear Creek Nature Center: Mountain Scrub, Coyote Gulch, and Creek Bottom Trails Loop

This excellent easy hike wanders through grassy meadows, Gambel oak groves, and lush creekside terrain while experiencing local wildlife and plants at Bear Creek Nature Center in Bear Creek Regional Park.

Start: Bear Creek Trailhead
Distance: 1.25 miles
Hiking time: About 1 hour
Type of hike: Loop
Trail names: Mountain Scrub Loop, Coyote Gulch Loop, Creek Bottom Loop
Difficulty: Easy. Cumulative elevation gain is 182 feet.
Trail surface: Paved, gravel, and dirt trail
Best season: Mar through Nov; trails may be icy, snowpacked, or muddy in winter.
Other trail users: Mountain bikers, equestrians
Restrictions: Park hours are 5 a.m. to 11 p.m. Nature Center hours are 9 a.m. to 4 p.m. Tues through Sat. No fees or permits required. No dogs allowed. Stay on designated trails. Park in designated parking lots. No littering, alcoholic beverages, glass containers, smoking, camping, dumping, hunting, tree cutting, fires, fireworks, overnight parking, or discharge of firearms.
Maps: Bear Creek Regional Park map on El Paso County website; USGS Manitou Springs, Colorado Springs
Trail contacts: Bear Creek Nature Center, (719) 520-6387; El Paso County Parks, (719) 520-7529

Finding the trailhead: From I-25, take the Cimarron Street / US 24 exit (exit 141). Drive west on US 24 for 2.1 miles to 26th Street.

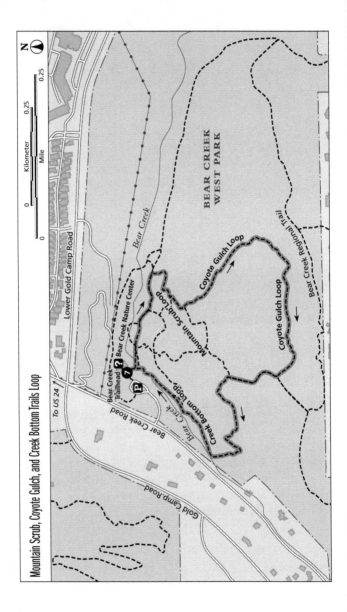

Mountain Scrub, Coyote Gulch, and Creek Bottom Trails Loop

Turn left (south) on 26th Street and go 1.4 miles (past the switch-backs) to a stop sign at Gold Camp Road. Go straight through the intersection onto Bear Creek Road. Drive down a short hill and turn left (east) after 0.2 mile into the Bear Creek Nature Center parking lot at 245 Bear Creek Road. GPS: 38.829285, -104.878877

The Hike

This superb loop hike at Bear Creek Nature Center, part of El Paso County's 575-acre Bear Creek Regional Park, links three trails that ring the outer perimeter of Bear Creek West. While the park's eastern side has a dog park, a playground, playing fields, a community garden, and an archery range, the park's west area offers natural habitats, including grassy meadows, scrubby foothills, and a riparian zone along sparkling Bear Creek. The hike offers tranquility and few hikers on the western edge of Colorado Springs.

Tucked against the Front Range and Red Rock Canyon Open Space, the Bear Creek Nature Center area is home to many bird species including woodpeckers, nuthatches, Stellar's jays, meadowlarks, turkeys, golden eagles, and great horned owls. Other common wildlife are mule deer, red foxes, ground squirrels, and garter snakes. Before hiking, check out the nature center, which offers information about local ecosystems, dioramas, and interactive exhibits that are ideal for youngsters, as well as guided hikes and interpretive programs (check beforehand for availability).

The first 0.1 mile of the hike, following a paved section of the Bear Creek Regional Trail, is wheelchair accessible. Also, just off that hike section is the 0.1-mile Songbird Trail, another accessible trail that is a VIP (Visually Impaired Persons) Trail. Informational signs are scattered along the trail.

Labels in the upper right corner of each sign can be touched with an audio device, which plays a recording of the sign's text.

The trails are well marked with map signs at each important junction and offer scenic views of the Front Range, including Tenney Crags, Mount Arthur, and Cheyenne Mountain, and of downtown Colorado Springs' skyline. Interpretive signs and benches line the route. Parts of the hike may be icy in winter and muddy after rainstorms.

The hike begins at a plaza on the west side of the Bear Creek Nature Center and follows a paved trail south across a bridge over Bear Creek, an important drainage that originates on the southwest side of Pikes Peak. The upper part of the creek is protected as the last refuge of the only remaining genetically pure population of indigenous greenback cutthroat trout.

From the bridge, hike east on the Bear Creek Trail and take a right onto the Mountain Scrub Loop, which climbs through a Gambel oak forest to a sloping grassy plain. Pick up the Coyote Gulch Loop here and go left, making an open loop through oak groves and shallow valleys before descending the plain to a junction with the Creek Bottom Loop. Go left on it and descend to tall cottonwoods shading Bear Creek and the hike's end at the center.

Miles and Directions

0.0   Begin at the Bear Creek Trailhead on the south side of the Bear Creek Nature Center. Walk south on the paved trail.

0.05 Reach a trail junction (GPS: 38.829042, -104.878749). Go left over a wooden bridge and hike east on the wide trail.

0.06 Pass a junction on the left with the Songbird Trail. Continue east past the next junction with the Songbird Trail.

0.2 Reach a junction with the Mountain Scrub Loop on the right (GPS: 38.828707, -104.875991). Go right on it and climb north-facing slopes covered with Gambel oak.

0.25 Pass a junction on the right with a connector trail and continue straight.

0.3 Reach a junction with the Coyote Gulch Loop at the top of the hill (GPS: 38.827928, -104.876991). Go left on the Coyote Gulch Loop and hike through meadows and oak groves.

0.45 The trail drops into wooded Coyote Gulch and passes two junctions on the left with connector trails to the Bear Creek Regional Trail. Continue straight on the main trail.

0.75 Reach a junction with a connector trail on the left above a broad meadow (GPS: 38.825712, -104.879051). Keep right on the Coyote Gulch Loop and hike north through the meadow.

0.85 Reach a junction with the Creek Bottom Loop at the north side of the meadow (GPS: 38.826887, -104.879062). Go left on the Creek Bottom Loop and start hiking downhill. Lower down, the trail descends timber steps and reaches the edge of Bear Creek. Hike north along the creek below tall cottonwoods, passing a connector trail on the right.

1.22 Cross a wooden bridge and reach the first trail junction south of the nature center. Go straight on the paved trail.

1.25 Arrive back at the trailhead (GPS: 38.829285, -104.878877).

8 North Cheyenne Cañon Park: Lower Columbine Trail

This pleasant hike follows the Lower Columbine Trail along the south bank of North Cheyenne Creek, passing below towering granite cliffs and pinnacles in the lower canyon to a turn-around spot at the start of the Middle Columbine Trail.

Start: Lower Columbine Trail Trailhead
Distance: 2.0 miles
Hiking time: About 1 hour
Type of hike: Out and back
Trail name: Lower Columbine Trail
Difficulty: Easy. Cumulative elevation gain is 320 feet.
Trail surface: Single-track and double-track dirt and rock trail
Best season: May through Oct, but the trail is open year-round. Bring micro spikes for traction and trekking poles in winter since the trail can be icy.
Other trail users: Mountain bikers
Restrictions: Park hours are 5 a.m. to 10 p.m. May through Oct, 5 a.m. to 9 p.m. Nov through Apr. Gates close nightly on North

Cheyenne Cañon Road at Starsmore Nature and Visitor Center and on Gold Camp Road. Leashed dogs allowed; pet waste must be promptly picked up and disposed of by the pet owner. Stay on designated trails. Park in designated areas and parking lots. No littering, alcoholic beverages, smoking, camping, dumping, tree cutting, or fires.
Maps: Colorado Springs Parks, Recreation and Cultural Services website; USGS Manitou Springs
Trail contacts: Colorado Springs Parks, Recreation and Cultural Services, (719) 385-5940; Starsmore Nature and Visitor Center, (719) 385-6086

Finding the trailhead: From I-25, take the Nevada Avenue / CO 115 exit (exit 140). Drive south on South Tejon Street for 0.4 mile

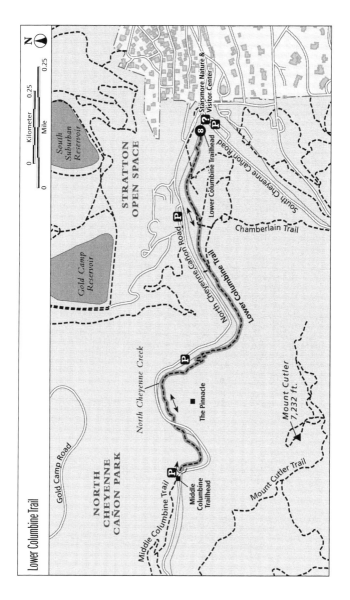

Lower Columbine Trail

to a roundabout. Take the second right off the roundabout and drive west on Cheyenne Boulevard for 2.6 miles, passing intersections with 8th Street and Cresta Road and an inverted Y junction with Cheyenne Road, to the start of North Cheyenne Cañon on the road. Keep left over a stone bridge and park in a large lot opposite the Starsmore Nature and Visitor Center. Walk up a short road to the front of the visitor center and the trailhead on the left. GPS: 38.790926, -104.865091

The Hike

The Columbine Trail, running 4 miles from the Starsmore Nature and Visitor Center to the Powell Parking Lot at the end of North Cheyenne Cañon Road, is divided into three distinct segments—the Lower, Middle, and Upper Columbine Trails. This superb hike, following the Lower Columbine Trail, threads along the south bank of North Cheyenne Creek into North Cheyenne Cañon, a narrow gorge walled with towering cliffs composed of pink Pikes Peak granite, to a turn-around point at a parking lot at the start of the Middle Columbine Trail.

North Cheyenne Cañon Park, a Colorado Springs city parkland since 1885, has long been a popular excursion for hikers and explorers. Early residents brought visitors here by carriage to marvel at the granite skyscrapers and rushing creek. In 1893 a writer praised the canyon in a travel book, writing: "This canyon abounds in beautiful waterfalls and cascades. . . . Beautiful, picturesque, grand, and in places awe-inspiring, are these stupendous gorges, awakening deepest emotions in all beholders." Take this easy hike and you will also gush about the canyon's natural wonders and beauty.

The trail is easy to follow, with signs at strategic junctions and a solid footbed of compacted dirt and occasional rocks. Part of the trail follows an old, closed road. Kids and families love the shady hike on hot days, wading adventures in the sparkling creek, and educational displays and programs at Starsmore. The trail passes through thick Gambel oak groves to tall ponderosa pines spilling down steep slopes above. Watch for wildlife, including mule deer, Abert's squirrels, and many birds like kingfishers and American dippers. In summer, look for hummingbirds along the trail and at the nature center.

The lower canyon offers established climbing routes for experienced rock climbers, including the classic Army Route first done by 10th Mountain Division climbers during World War II. All climbers must be registered and use proper equipment.

Miles and Directions

0.0 Start at the front of the Starsmore Nature and Visitor Center. Go left on a paved trail around the south side of the stone building. Pass a trail sign and go through a gate.

0.05 Reach a junction west of the center and go left on the Lower Columbine Trail.

0.2 Reach a junction and continue straight on the trail (GPS: 38.790903, -104.868866).

0.6 Reach a junction with a trail on the left before a stone bridge and parking lot (GPS: 38.790842, -104.874246). Go left on the trail and hike up three switchbacks. Continue northwest on the trail, passing below The Pinnacle, a towering rocky cliff.

0.85 Pass a stone bridge and reach the park road (GPS: 38.791737,-104.877032). Cross at a crosswalk onto the west side of the road and continue west on the trail.

1.0 Arrive at the hike's turn-around point at a parking lot and the Middle Columbine Trailhead (GPS: 38.791560, -104.879014). Return from here down the Lower Columbine Trail.

2.0 Arrive back at the trailhead (GPS: 38.790926, -104.865091).

9 North Cheyenne Cañon Park: Mount Cutler Trail

The trail climbs through a pine and fir forest in North Cheyenne Cañon Park to the summit of 7,232-foot Mount Cutler, which offers panoramic views of Colorado Springs.

Start: Mount Cutler / Mount Muscoco Trailhead
Distance: 2.0 miles
Hiking time: About 1 hour
Type of hike: Out and back
Trail name: Mount Cutler Trail
Difficulty: Moderate. Cumulative elevation gain is 479 feet.
Trail surface: Single-track dirt trail
Best season: Apr through Nov; icy in winter
Other trail users: Hikers only
Restrictions: Park hours are 5 a.m. to 10 p.m. May through Oct, 5 a.m. to 9 p.m. Nov through Apr. Gates close nightly on North Cheyenne Cañon Road at Starsmore Nature and Visitor Center

and on Gold Camp Road. Leashed dogs allowed; pet waste must be promptly picked up and disposed of by the pet owner. Stay on designated trails. Park in designated areas and parking lots. No littering, alcoholic beverages, smoking, camping, dumping, tree cutting, or fires.
Maps: Colorado Springs Parks, Recreation and Cultural Services website; USGS Manitou Springs
Trail contacts: Colorado Springs Parks, Recreation and Cultural Services, (719) 385-5940; Starsmore Nature and Visitor Center, (719) 385-6086

Finding the trailhead: From I-25, take the Nevada Avenue / CO 115 exit (exit 140) and take the first right on South Tejon Street. Drive south on South Tejon for 0.4 mile to a roundabout. Take the second right off the roundabout and drive west on Cheyenne Boulevard for 2.6 miles, passing intersections with 8th Street and Cresta Road and an inverted Y junction with Cheyenne Road, to a Y junction at the mouth of North Cheyenne Cañon at the Starsmore Nature and Visitor Center. Go right through a gate and follow North Cheyenne Cañon Road for 1.4 miles to a parking lot at the Mount Cutler Trailhead on the left. GPS: 38.791810, -104.887147

The Hike

North Cheyenne Cañon, protected in a 1,276-acre Colorado Springs city park, slices through the rugged Front Range on the city's southwest side. North Cheyenne Cañon Road twists west into this spectacular canyon, passing towering

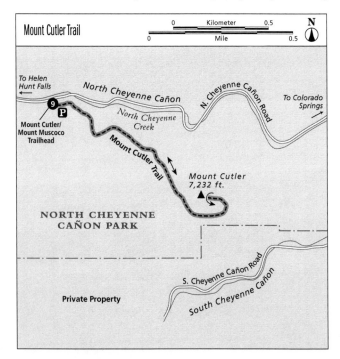

granite cliffs and slopes blanketed with white fir, Douglas fir, and ponderosa pine and offering access to a comprehensive trail network in the park and surrounding Pike National Forest. Mount Cutler is named for Henry Cutler, a nineteenth-century New England philanthropist who provided funding for Colorado College.

Towering above the lower canyon, cliff-lined Mount Cutler offers the easiest and most accessible summit climb in the Pikes Peak region. The Mount Cutler Trail threads up the mountain's northwest slope, gently rising through forest to a junction with the Mount Muscoco Trail. From here the airy trail swings across the top of Cutler's rocky southwest face, edging across an exposed slope, with steep cliffs and drop-offs to your right. From this section, look down right to glimpse Seven Falls cascading far below. Finish by scrambling up gravel slopes to the mountain's rounded summit and panoramic views across North and South Cheyenne Cañons, the sprawling city, and distant tawny plains.

Watch children as you hike along the exposed trail above South Cheyenne Cañon, especially if you make the extra-credit hike out to the lower east summit, which perches above dangerous vertical cliffs. Some of the footing on the upper slopes is on loose gravel scattered atop the granite bedrock.

Also, be careful if you hike Mount Cutler in winter. The first trail section to the junction with the Mount Muscoco Trail is usually snowpacked and icy. Bring boot traction like micro spikes and trekking poles for safety.

Miles and Directions

0.0   Begin at the Mount Cutler / Mount Muscoco Trailhead on the west side of the parking area. Hike up the trail, steadily climbing up wooded slopes.

0.4   Arrive at an overlook with views down North Cheyenne Cañon to the Colorado Springs skyline. Continue up the trail, passing cliffs above the trail.

0.5   Reach a saddle at a tall ponderosa pine and the junction with the Mount Muscoco Trail on the right (GPS: 38.788101, -104.879245). Continue straight on the Mount Cutler Trail and hike across the peak's rocky southwest flank. Watch for drop-offs. At an obvious junction, go left and hike up gentle slopes.

1.0   Arrive at the summit of Mount Cutler (GPS: 38.787892, -104.877828). Retrace your steps down the trail.

2.0   Arrive back at the trailhead (GPS: 38.791810, -104.887147).

Option: To reach Mount Cutler's lower east summit, go left (east) from the main trail on one of two trails just below the main summit. A short distance east of the main path, these two trails join. Follow the trail another 0.25 mile east to Cutler's lower summit. This lofty perch, surrounded by airy cliffs, yields superb views of Colorado Springs and the Broadmoor Hotel area below. Some of the footing is loose, and parts of the trail are above vertical cliffs. Keep children close and pets leashed for safety.

10 North Cheyenne Cañon Park: Silver Cascade Falls and Buffalo Canyon Trails

This scenic loop hike passes two gorgeous waterfalls—Helen Hunt Falls and Silver Cascade Falls—in North Cheyenne Cañon on the southwest edge of Colorado Springs.

Start: Silver Cascade Falls Trailhead
Distance: 0.95 mile
Hiking time: About 1 hour
Type of hike: Loop
Trail names: Silver Cascade Falls Trail, Buffalo Canyon Trail
Difficulty: Moderate. Cumulative elevation gain is 367 feet.
Trail surface: Single-track dirt trail
Best season: Apr through Oct; icy in winter
Other trail users: Hikers only
Restrictions: Park hours are 5 a.m. to 10 p.m. May through Oct, 5 a.m. to 9 p.m. Nov through Apr. Gates close nightly on North Cheyenne Cañon Road at Starsmore Nature and Visitor Center

and on Gold Camp Road. Leashed dogs allowed; pet waste must be promptly picked up and disposed of by the pet owner. Stay on designated trails. Park in designated areas and parking lots. No littering, alcoholic beverages, smoking, camping, dumping, tree cutting, or fires.
Maps: Colorado Springs Parks, Recreation and Cultural Services website; USGS Manitou Springs
Trail contacts: Colorado Springs Parks, Recreation and Cultural Services, (719) 385-5940; Starsmore Nature and Visitor Center, (719) 385-6086

Finding the trailhead: From I-25, take the Nevada Avenue / CO 115 exit (exit 140). Drive south on South Tejon Street for 0.4 mile

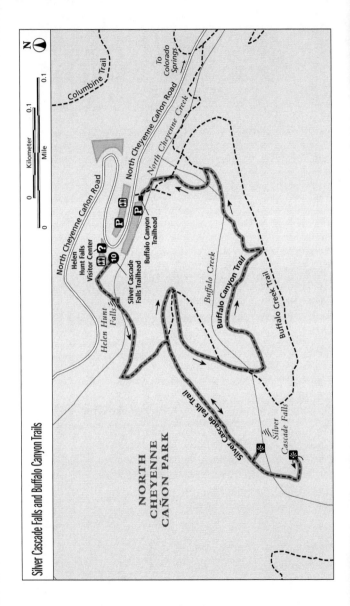

Silver Cascade Falls and Buffalo Canyon Trails

to a roundabout. Take the second right off the roundabout and drive west on Cheyenne Boulevard for 2.6 miles, passing intersections with 8th Street and Cresta Road and an inverted Y junction with Cheyenne Road, to a Y junction at the Starsmore Nature and Visitor Center. Go right on North Cheyenne Cañon Road and drive 2.5 miles west up the canyon to parking lots at the Helen Hunt Falls Visitor Center. The Silver Cascade Falls Trailhead is left of the visitor center. GPS: 38.788805, -104.903070

The Hike

This short loop hike discovers two waterfalls and gives spectacular views of rugged North Cheyenne Cañon and Mount Muscoco to the east. The hike begins at a trailhead beside the Helen Hunt Falls Visitor Center and next to 36-foot Helen Hunt Falls. The center, open in summer only, offers information, exhibits, hiking tips, and educational programs. The hike lies within North Cheyenne Cañon Park, a Colorado Springs city park.

Use caution on the trail, especially in winter. The first section past Helen Hunt Falls is usually icy and snowpacked. Bring micro spikes and trekking poles for balance and traction. The hike's most dangerous section is the smooth slab that Silver Cascade Falls tumbles down. Do not venture onto the slab. It's slippery, water polished, and steeper than it looks. The upper trail section is fenced for your safety. Severe injuries and fatalities have occurred here.

Start by hiking up stone steps to a bridge above Helen Hunt Falls. This pretty waterfall, filled with snowmelt in May and June, is named for famed nineteenth-century author and poet Helen Hunt Jackson, who often sat at the falls for inspiration in the 1870s. After dying of cancer in 1885, she was buried in nearby South Cheyenne Cañon before being reinterred at Evergreen Cemetery in Colorado Springs.

The next hike segment climbs to a view point above Silver Cascade Falls. Buffalo Creek, rising on Mount Rosa to the west, feeds the waterfall, which cascades almost 200 feet down a granite slab. An overlook ringed by a stone wall perches above the waterfall and is the turn-around point for this hike section.

The last segment returns down to a junction and goes right on the Buffalo Canyon Trail, which descends gravel slopes to the base of Silver Cascade Falls. Continue along the trail beside Buffalo Creek to a junction and go left to a trailhead at the east end of the parking lot.

Miles and Directions

0.0 Begin at the Silver Cascade Falls Trailhead on the left side of the Helen Hunt Falls Visitor Center (GPS: 38.788805, -104.903070). Climb a stone staircase and cross a bridge over the top of Helen Hunt Falls. Continue up the trail, crossing a slope above North Cheyenne Creek.

0.1 Reach a junction with the Buffalo Creek Trail on the left (GPS: 38.788189, -104.904059). Continue up the Silver Cascade Falls Trail above a granite slab. The trail is fenced on the left to keep hikers off the slab.

0.3 Arrive at a rock-walled overlook above Silver Cascade Falls (GPS: 38.787256, -104.905576). After admiring the waterfall, descend the trail. *Caution:* Do not scramble down the slabs below the overlook and trail. The granite is slick, dangerous, and fatalities have occurred here.

0.4 Reach the junction on the right with the Buffalo Canyon Trail. Go right on it and hike east on a gravel ridge with good views of Silver Cascade Falls. Descend to the base of the waterfall. Continue down the trail beside Buffalo Creek in Buffalo Canyon. At a junction, go left to a bridge over North Cheyenne Creek and reach the Buffalo Canyon Trailhead by the road.

0.95 Arrive at the Buffalo Canyon Trailhead about 100 feet east of the visitor center (GPS: 38.788539, -104.902295).

11 Cheyenne Mountain State Park: Coyote Run Trail

This fun hike in Cheyenne Mountain State Park explores the hills above the park's visitor center, passing open meadows, Gambel oak forests, and scattered ponderosa pines.

Start: Coyote Run Trailhead
Distance: 1.5 miles
Hiking time: About 1 hour
Type of hike: Lollipop loop
Trail name: Coyote Run Trail
Difficulty: Easy. Cumulative elevation gain is 153 feet.
Trail surface: Dirt trail
Best season: Apr through Nov; trail is usually dry in winter.
Other trail users: Mountain bikers
Restrictions: Fee area. Pay daily fee at visitor center, entrance station booth, or kiosk. Park hours are 5 a.m. to 10 p.m. Visitor center open daily 9 a.m. to 4 p.m. Oct through Apr, 9 a.m. to 5 p.m. May through Sept. Leashed dogs allowed; pet waste must be picked up by the pet owner. Stay on designated trails. Park in designated parking lots. Dispose of waste properly. Respect wildlife. No littering, alcoholic beverages, smoking, dumping, tree cutting, or fires. Park campground is open year-round.
Maps: Cheyenne Mountain State Park website; USGS Cheyenne Mountain
Trail contact: Cheyenne Mountain State Park, (719) 576-2016

Finding the trailhead: From I-25, take the South Academy Boulevard exit (exit 135) and drive west on South Academy past Pikes Peak State College. Continue west and turn south onto CO 115. Drive south for 1.9 miles on the divided highway to a stoplight opposite Fort Carson Gate 1. Turn right on JL Ranch Heights Road, signed for Cheyenne Mountain State Park, and drive west for 0.7 mile to the park visitor center on the right. Park in the visitor center lot.

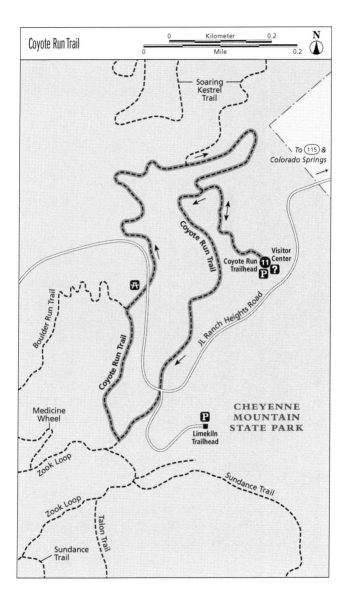

Coyote Run Trail

Soaring Kestrel Trail

Kilometer
0   0.2
Mile
0   0.2

N

To (115) &
Colorado Springs

Coyote Run Trail

Coyote Run Trail

Visitor Center

Coyote Run Trailhead

11 P ?

JL Ranch Heights Road

Boulder Run Trail

Coyote Run Trail

Medicine Wheel

P
Limekiln Trailhead

CHEYENNE MOUNTAIN STATE PARK

Zook Loop

Sundance Trail

Zook Loop

Talon Trail

Sundance Trail

The Coyote Run Trailhead is on the west side of the parking lot at a kiosk. Park address: 410 JL Ranch Heights Road. GPS: 38.734986, -104.819778

The Hike

The Coyote Run Trail is a splendid hike for kids and families in the foothills above the Cheyenne Mountain State Park Visitor Center, which makes a fun stop with its informative displays about the park's natural history. The easy-to-follow single-track trail has minimal elevation gain, gradual grades, and plenty of rest stops. It's well marked with signposts at regular intervals.

Start the hike on the west side of the visitor center parking lot. The trailhead is between two benches left of a kiosk with park information. Hike west to a Y junction in a garden of granite boulders and the start of the Coyote Run loop trail. Go left (south) to begin the loop.

The next segment runs south, crossing the park road at its turnoff to the Limekiln Trailhead, to a junction with the Zook Loop. Go right here for a few feet, then head right on Coyote Run. The trail climbs to a junction with the Boulder Run Trail. Keep right on Coyote Run and walk past picnic tables to a building and the park road. Following signs with arrows pointing the way, walk along the right (east) side of the building on a sidewalk. Cross the road to its east side to another building and parking lot. Go left and cross the road into the parking lot and pick up the Coyote Run Trail. Sounds confusing, but it's straightforward.

The last segment heads northeast to a junction with the Soaring Kestrel Trail and then descends to the first trail junction near the visitor center, passing a sign about rattlesnakes.

Prairie rattlers live in the park but are rarely seen. These warm, rocky slopes form an ideal habitat for rattlesnakes.

Miles and Directions

0.0 Start at the Coyote Run Trailhead on the west side of the visitor center parking lot and hike west. Gently ascend grassy slopes to a garden of rounded granite boulders.

0.1 Reach a junction at the start of the loop trail (GPS: 38.736016, -104.820488). Go left and hike southwest through Gambel oak thickets and meadows.

0.45 Reach the north side of the park road (GPS: 38.732661, -104.821687) at the turnoff to the Limekiln Trailhead and parking lot. Cross at a crosswalk at the intersection, pick up the Coyote Run Trail on the road's south side, and hike southwest on gentle slopes.

0.6 Reach a T junction with the Zook Loop Trail (GPS: 38.731492, -104.823387). Go right on it for 35 feet, then keep right on the Coyote Run Trail and hike north uphill through Gambel oak groves, pines, and scattered boulders.

0.85 Reach a junction with the Boulder Run Trail on the left (GPS: 38.734152, -104.823606). Keep right and hike northeast to a building. Pass it on the right on a sidewalk next to the park road and reach a crosswalk. Cross the road to a sidewalk.

1.0 After a few feet the sidewalk ends with a building to the right and a parking lot for a picnic area. Go left and cross the entrance road to the parking lot at a crosswalk to an informal trailhead for the Coyote Run Trail (GPS: 38.734890, -104.822135). Walk 40 feet to a junction and go left on the trail parallel to the road. Hike north through ponderosa pines, then bend east across open slopes and oak groves.

1.3 Past a group of large boulders, reach a junction with the Soaring Kestrel Trail (GPS: 38.737001, -104.820271). Keep right and bend south, then begin hiking downhill.

1.4 Reach the first trail junction in boulders and the end of the loop trail (GPS: 38.736016, -104.820488). Go left and hike southeast above the visitor center.

1.5 Arrive back at the trailhead (GPS: 38.734986, -104.819778).

12 Cheyenne Mountain State Park: Zook Loop Trail

The Zook Loop Trail is a fun, family-friendly hike with minimal elevation gain, an open woodland of Gambel oaks and ponderosa pines, and a shady bench at the halfway point.

Start: Limekiln Trailhead
Distance: 1.1 miles
Hiking time: About 1 hour
Type of hike: Lollipop loop
Trail name: Zook Loop Trail
Difficulty: Easy. Cumulative elevation gain is 126 feet.
Trail surface: Dirt trail
Best season: Apr through Nov; parts of trail are icy in winter.
Other trail users: Mountain bikers
Restrictions: Fee area. Pay daily fee at visitor center, entrance station booth, or kiosk. Park hours are 5 a.m. to 10 p.m. Visitor center open daily 9 a.m. to 4 p.m. Oct through Apr, 9 a.m. to 5 p.m. May through Sept. Leashed dogs allowed; pet waste must be picked up by the pet owner. Stay on designated trails. Park in designated parking lots. Dispose of waste properly. Respect wildlife. No littering, alcoholic beverages, smoking, dumping, tree cutting, or fires. Park campground is open year-round.
Maps: Cheyenne Mountain State Park website and trailhead; USGS Cheyenne Mountain
Trail contacts: Cheyenne Mountain State Park, (719) 576-2016

Finding the trailhead: From I-25, take the South Academy Boulevard exit (exit 135) and drive west on South Academy past Pikes Peak State College. Continue west and turn south onto CO 115. Drive south for 1.9 miles on the divided highway to a stoplight opposite Fort Carson Gate 1. Turn right on JL Ranch Heights Road, signed for Cheyenne Mountain State Park, and drive west for 0.7 mile to the park visitor center on the right. Continue southwest on the park road for 0.3 mile,

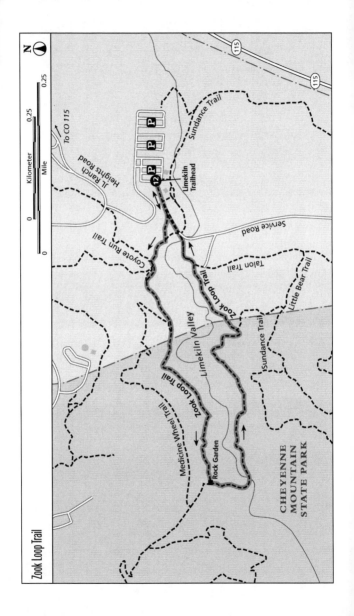

passing the entrance station and fee kiosk, and turn left toward the signed Limekiln Trailhead. Drive 0.2 mile and turn right into a large parking lot. The Limekiln Trailhead is on the west side of the parking lot and right of the restrooms. Park address: 410 JL Ranch Heights. GPS: 38.731298, -104.821439

The Hike

The Zook Loop Trail explores shallow Limekiln Valley, traversing gentle grass-covered hillsides and threading through Gambel oak groves and scattered ponderosa pines. The hike, ideal for children, has minimal elevation gain, is signed with round blue trail markers, and is one of the best easy day hikes in the Colorado Springs area. The single-track path, shared with mountain bikers, offers solitude, wildlife, and great views of rugged Cheyenne Mountain towering to the west. Shaded by tall pines, the Rock Garden at the halfway point is the hike's highlight. Sit among its rounded granite boulders and enjoy birdsong and the whisper of wind.

The trail can be hiked in either a clockwise or counterclockwise direction. This description goes counterclockwise. Begin at the Limekiln Trailhead, the park's largest trailhead, and hike west from the restrooms to a junction and go right. Following blue markers, the trail crosses grassy slopes broken with oak groves to the Rock Garden. The return section follows slopes on the south side of the valley. This segment holds snow, ice, and mud in winter, so bring micro spikes and trekking poles for balance.

Cheyenne Mountain State Park sprawls across 2,701 acres between Highway 115 and 9,164-foot Dragon's Backbone, the eastern subsummit of Cheyenne Mountain. Over 27 miles on twenty-one trails twist through the park on varied terrain from rolling grassland to steep canyons and rocky peaks, providing plenty of adventures for hikers of all abilities. The park also has a visitor center with educational displays, guided hikes, ranger-led programs, and a sixty-one-site campground. Dogs are not allowed on trails except four short ones by the campground.

Miles and Directions

0.0 Start at the Limekiln Trailhead right of the restrooms at the west side of the parking lot. Hike west on the wide trail.

0.05 Reach a Y junction and go right on the Zook Loop Trail, which is designated with a circular blue sign labeled "Zook Trail." Hike northwest across a grassy meadow.

0.1 Reach a junction on the right with the Coyote Run Trail (GPS: 38.731499, -104.823401). Keep left on the Zook Loop Trail and immediately pass another junction for the Coyote Run Trail, which goes right. Continue straight on the Zook Loop Trail and hike west past granite boulders and Gambel oak groves. Pass a junction on the right with the Medicine Wheel Trail and continue west.

0.5 Reach the midpoint of the hike at the Rock Garden, a grove of ponderosa pines towering over boulders (GPS: 38.730195, -104.829459). Stop at a shady bench, read an interpretive sign about black bears, and enjoy this quiet spot. A junction with the Medicine Wheel Trail is right of the sign. Continue hiking on the Zook Loop Trail, bending south across a dry creek bed in Limekiln Valley.

0.55 Pass a junction on the right with an unnamed trail. Continue straight, hiking east on the valley's south edge through a woodland of Gambel oaks, ponderosa pines, and occasional Douglas firs.

0.85 Reach a junction on the right with the Sundance Trail (GPS: 38.729519, -104.825316). Keep left on the Zook Loop Trail and begin descending across open terrain with good views of Cheyenne Mountain.

0.95 Pass a junction with the Talon Trail on the right (GPS: 38.730507, -104.823500). Continue straight on the Zook Loop Trail, crossing a bridge over a dry creek and passing the start of the Sundance Trail on the right and a spur to the left.

1.05 Pass the start of the Zook Loop Trail and hike east.

1.1 Arrive back at the trailhead (GPS: 38.731298, -104.821439).

13 Fountain Creek Regional Park: Fountain Creek Nature Trail

This short loop hike explores wildlife-rich ponds and wetlands at the Cattail Marsh Wildlife Area south of Colorado Springs.

Start: Fountain Creek Nature Trailhead
Distance: 0.7 mile
Hiking time: 30 minutes to 1 hour
Type of hike: Loop
Trail name: Fountain Creek Nature Trail
Difficulty: Easy. Cumulative elevation gain is 31 feet. The trail is stroller friendly when dry.
Trail surface: Double-track dirt trail
Best season: Apr through Nov; open year-round
Other trail users: Hikers only
Restrictions: Trails are open from dawn to dusk. Nature center hours are 9 a.m. to 4 p.m. Tues through Sat. No fees or permits required. No dogs, horses, bicycles, or fishing allowed in the wildlife area. Stay on designated trails. Park in designated parking lots. No littering, alcoholic beverages, glass containers, smoking, camping, dumping, hunting, tree cutting, fires, fireworks, overnight parking, or discharge of firearms.
Maps: El Paso County Parks website; USGS Fountain
Trail contacts: El Paso County Parks & Community Services, (719) 520-7529; Fountain Creek Nature Center, (719) 520-6745

Finding the trailhead: Drive south on I-25 from Colorado Springs to the Mesa Ridge Parkway / CO 16 exit (exit 132). Turn left (east) at the light onto Mesa Ridge Parkway / CO 16 and drive 0.7 mile to US 85/87. Turn right (south) onto US 85/87 and drive south for 0.6 mile to a right (west) turn onto Cattail Marsh Road, signed for Fountain Creek Nature Center. Follow the dirt road for 0.2 mile to a parking lot. The trailhead is on the south side of the lot. Nature center street address: 320 Peppergrass Lane, Fountain. GPS: 38.713644, -104.716641

The Hike

The Fountain Creek Nature Trail loops through the Cattail Marsh Wildlife Area along the east side of Fountain Creek. The trail explores cattail-lined ponds and wetlands that offer crucial habitat for wildlife. The trail, accessible to strollers when dry, is mostly flat, with only slight hills at the start and finish. The year-round hike affords a much

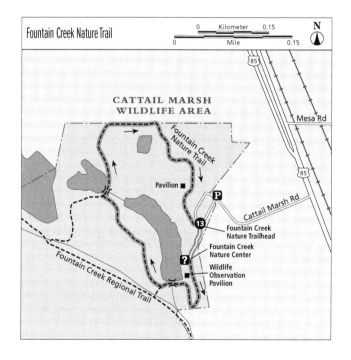

different experience from the mountain trails west of Colorado Springs.

The Cattail Marsh Wildlife Area is a lowland riparian ecosystem, one of Colorado's most species-rich habitats. The area's ponds, once gravel pits, lie on the floodplain of Fountain Creek, which rises from snowmelt on Pikes Peak and drains into the Arkansas River in Pueblo.

The wildlife area is a quiet preserve for many animals and an outdoor classroom for visitors of all ages. At least 310 species of birds, mammals, reptiles, and amphibians share this habitat, including white-tailed deer, raccoon, beaver, muskrat, red fox, garter snake, bull snake, tiger salamander, painted turtle, and leopard frog. The area is also the best bird-watching site in the Pikes Peak region, with over 270 species spotted here. Common birds seen are red-winged blackbird, Canada goose, great blue heron, mallard and wood ducks, kingfisher, red-tailed hawk, and turkey vulture.

Start the hike at the trailhead on the south end of the parking lot and follow a concrete trail to the Fountain Creek Nature Center, which perches on the hill above the ponds. Inside the pavilion are displays that describe the area's natural history, rich human history, and the importance of wetlands. Interpretive signs are scattered along the trail. Take time to read them as you hike and learn more about this natural area. You can also enrich your experience by taking a guided audio tour and scanning QR codes at nine locations along the trail.

The Nature Trail descends to the Cattail Marsh wetland below, passing ponds, marshes, benches, towering cottonwood trees, and open meadows. Keep alert for white-tailed deer, which often graze below the trees. Bring binoculars to spot red-winged blackbirds perched on cattails, great blue herons wading in shallow waters, and turtles sunning on fallen logs. Take note of a giant, gnarled cottonwood dubbed Grandfather Cottonwood, one of the largest specimens in the Pikes Peak region. The tree is over 170 years old, as tall as a five-story building, and has a girth exceeding 20 feet at its base. Remember to pause alongside the large pond, its still water reflecting blue sky and clouds. Listen for the croak of bullfrogs and the smack of carp feeding at the pond's surface.

Near the end of the hike is an open meadow filled with milkweed and a view of distant Pikes Peak. This habitat is a designated Monarch Way Station, a stopping-off place for migrating monarch butterflies. The monarchs come in August and September, when the caterpillars feed only on the white juice, or milk, of the milkweed. The plant is toxic to mammals and birds, so after feasting on the milk, the butterflies become unappetizing to birds.

Miles and Directions

0.0 Start at the Fountain Creek Nature Trailhead on the south side of the parking lot and left of a kiosk with park information (GPS: 38.713644, -104.716641). Walk south on a concrete sidewalk.

0.02 Reach the front doors of the Fountain Creek Nature Center on the right. Learn about the park's natural history, the Fountain Creek drainage, and area history in the center before setting off on the trail. Continue south on the concrete trail, which turns to dirt past the center, and pass a wildlife observation pavilion on the right. The pavilion offers views across the Cattail Marsh Wildlife Area below, a spotting scope, and tips for wildlife watching. Descend the trail south and then west into the wildlife area.

0.2 Cross a bridge over a pond's outlet stream and reach a junction on the left with a spur path to the Fountain Creek Regional Trail (GPS: 38.712539, -104.717605). Continue straight on the Fountain Creek Nature Trail, which bends right and runs northwest alongside marshy terrain, passing beneath massive Grandfather Cottonwood.

0.35 Reach a junction with a longer spur on the left that goes to the Fountain Creek Regional Trail (GPS: 38.714194, -104.719006). Stay right on the Fountain Creek Nature Trail and cross a bridge over a marsh between two ponds. Continue north past more tall cottonwoods and bend right on the trail. Hike east on the level trail between a grassland on the left and a cattail marsh on the right with a viewing platform. The trail turns right and passes the Monarch Way Station.

0.65 Reach a pavilion on the right used for park educational programs. Continue south on the wide trail, gently climbing a wooded embankment.

0.7 Arrive back at a trailhead on the southwest corner of the parking lot (GPS: 38.713687, -104.7167510).

14 Clear Spring Ranch Open Space: Clear Spring Ranch Loop

This loop hike explores the cottonwood bosque along the west bank of Clear Spring Ranch Open Space, an El Paso County parkland south of Colorado Springs.

Start: Clear Spring Ranch Trailhead

Distance: 0.85 mile

Hiking time: About 30 minutes

Type of hike: Lollipop loop

Trail name: Fountain Creek Regional Trail / Front Range Trail

Difficulty: Easy. Cumulative elevation gain is 13 feet.

Trail surface: Single-track and double-track dirt trail

Best season: Year-round; usually dry in winter

Other trail users: Mountain bikers, equestrians

Restrictions: Park open from dawn until dark. Farm fields and the homestead are closed to visitors and hikers. Leashed dogs allowed; pet waste must be picked up and disposed of by the pet owner. No harassment of wildlife or farm animals. Stay on designated trails. Park in designated parking lots. No littering, alcoholic beverages, glass containers, smoking, camping, dumping, hunting, tree cutting, fires, fireworks, overnight parking, or discharge of firearms. Restrooms in the picnic area are open year-round.

Maps: El Paso County map on website; USGS Buttes

Trail contact: El Paso County Parks, (719) 520-7529

Finding the trailhead: From Colorado Springs, drive south on I-25 and take exit 123. At the end of the exit ramp, turn left and drive through a single-lane tunnel under the highway, bump across railroad tracks, and, following signs, go left and then drive east on an unnamed dirt road for 0.2 mile to a large parking lot on the left and the trailhead. GPS: 38.611664, -104.677973

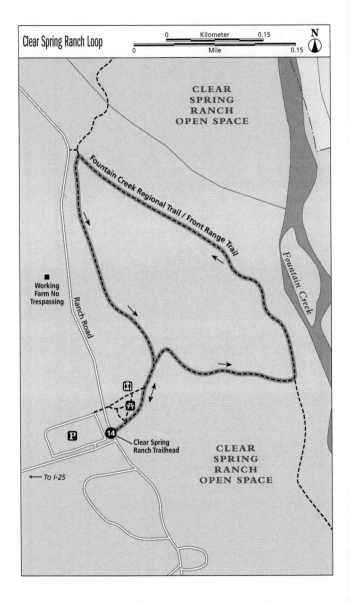

Clear Spring Ranch Loop

Kilometer
0   0.15

Mile
0   0.15

N

CLEAR
SPRING
RANCH
OPEN SPACE

Fountain Creek Regional Trail / Front Range Trail

Fountain Creek

Working
Farm No
Trespassing

Ranch Road

P

14

Clear Spring
Ranch Trailhead

← To I-25

CLEAR
SPRING
RANCH
OPEN SPACE

The Hike

Clear Spring Ranch Open Space, a 930-acre El Paso County parkland on Colorado Springs Utilities land, stretches alongside Fountain Creek south of the town of Fountain. The open space, once called Colorado Springs State Wildlife Area, offers 4 miles of hiking on the Fountain Creek Regional Trail, which is part of the Front Range Trail, a proposed 800-mile trail that will eventually link Colorado's major cities from Wyoming to New Mexico.

The open space protects a bosque ecosystem along the creek, with a mature riparian forest on Fountain Creek's floodplain. The plains cottonwood is the dominant tree here, depending on reliable groundwater for seed germination and survival in the dry climate. Reproducing by seed, cottonwoods spread their seeds by wind and water. The seeds germinate in springtime on bare soil that is often inundated by spring flooding. Add sunshine and warmth, and the seedlings thrive. The plains cottonwood, related to aspen trees, grows as tall as 100 feet with branches spreading to 60 feet. They usually live about 75 years, although some specimens here are probably 100 years old.

The bosque also provides valuable habitat for wildlife, including birds, mammals, and reptiles. Watch in summer for diverse bird species including songbirds, woodpeckers, geese, turkeys, and raptors like owls and hawks. Bald eagles are spotted in winter, and a pair of golden eagles often nest in the north part of the refuge. Reptiles include prairie rattlesnakes, which are seen in summer.

With its warm, dry weather, this easy loop makes a great winter hike. Summer days can be hot, but shade is found on the trail. Wear a hat and bring water. The hike begins at the parking lot and passes through a picnic area with a shady ramada and restrooms. It follows the Fountain Creek Trail to the creek, then cuts northwest to a junction and returns south past towering cottonwoods to the picnic area and trail's end.

Besides the bosque, Clear Spring Ranch Open Space also contains active farming areas. Stay out of the fields and the buildings south of the trailhead, and don't walk on the ranch roads.

Miles and Directions

0.0 Start at the unsigned trailhead on the east side of the parking lot. Walk across a ranch road and go through another gap in a wooden fence to the picnic area. Follow the trail along a fence past a kiosk with an open space map. Leave the picnic area and continue east.

0.1 Reach a junction (GPS: 38.612661, -104.677049) and keep right. The left trail is the return route. Hike east on the Fountain Creek Regional Trail through the bosque ecosystem. Pass interpretive signs about biological communities, animal tracks, and bird tree homes.

0.25 Reach a signed T junction on Fountain Creek's west bank (GPS: 38.612424, -104.674538). Go left on the Fountain Creek Regional Trail, also signed Front Range Trail. Follow the trail along the creek and then northwest past a sign about turkeys. Continue along a closed ranch road shaded by trees.

0.55 Reach a junction (GPS: 38.615474, -104.678429) and go sharply left. Hike south on the wide trail past massive cottonwood trees and a sign about prairie dogs.

0.75 Meet the first junction and go right. Hike through the picnic area and cross the ranch road.

0.85 Arrive back at the trailhead (GPS: 38.611664, -104.677973).

15 Ute Valley Park: Triple Treat, Rattlesnake Ridge, and Valley View Trails

These three trails offer an excellent lollipop loop hike that explores Rattlesnake Ridge, a high hogback on Ute Valley Park's western edge, and yields scenic views of 14,115-foot Pikes Peak and the Rampart Range to the west.

Start: Piñon Valley Park Trailhead
Distance: 1.95 miles
Hiking time: About 1 hour
Type of hike: Lollipop loop
Trail names: Triple Treat, Rattlesnake Ridge Trail, Valley View Trail
Difficulty: Moderate. Cumulative elevation gain is 267 feet.
Trail surface: Dirt road, dirt trail, rocky in sections
Best season: Mar through Nov; parts of hike can be icy in winter.
Other trail users: Mountain bikers
Restrictions: Park hours are 5 a.m. to 9 p.m. Nov through Apr, 5 a.m. to 10 p.m. May through Oct. Leashed dogs allowed; pet waste must be picked up by the pet owner. Stay on designated trails. No littering, alcoholic beverages, smoking, camping, dumping, tree cutting, or fires. No e-bikes or other motorized devices, including power scooters, hoverboards, electric skateboards, ATVs, motorcycles, and remote-control vehicles.
Maps: Colorado Springs Parks, Recreation and Cultural Services website; USGS Pikeview
Trail contact: Colorado Springs Parks, Recreation and Cultural Services, (719) 385-5940

Finding the trailhead: From I-25, take Garden of the Gods Road exit 146 and drive west for 1.1 miles to Centennial Boulevard. Turn right onto Centennial, drive north for 1.5 miles, and turn right on Mule Deer Drive. Follow Mule Deer Drive east to Piñon Valley Park and continue southeast alongside the park to Piñon Park Drive on the left

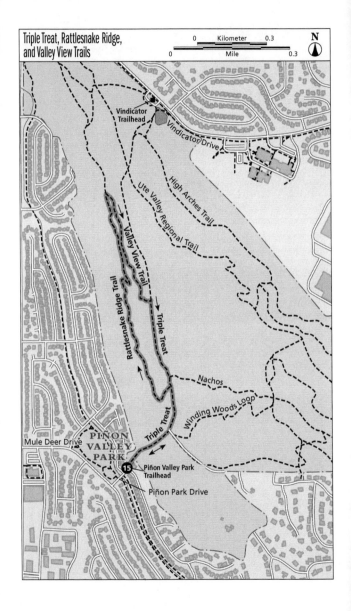

0   Kilometer   0.3

0   Mile   0.3

N

Vindicator Trailhead

Vindicator Drive

High Arches Trail

Ute Valley Regional Trail

Valley View Trail

Rattlesnake Ridge Trail

Triple Treat

Nachos

Winding Woods Loop

Mule Deer Drive

PIÑON VALLEY PARK

15

Piñon Valley Park Trailhead

Piñon Park Drive

Triple Treat

at the park's end. Park along the street beside Piñon Valley Park. The Piñon Valley Park Trailhead is at the gated end of Piñon Park Drive on the park boundary. GPS: 38.911278, -104.858175

The Hike

Surrounded by suburbs on the edge of the Rampart Range in northwest Colorado Springs, Ute Valley Park offers an urban enclave of wildlife, craggy bluffs and ridges, and an extensive network of trails for hikers of all abilities to discover. The 538-acre park offers a quick hiking getaway with wide trails, easy grades, and plenty of room to roam.

The park harbors a foothills ecosystem, a transition zone between mountains and plains with wildflower-strewn meadows and a diverse woodland of ponderosa pine, Gambel oak, juniper, and piñon pine. The park's barebones landscape is composed of sandstone, with Rattlesnake Ridge, its main geologic formation, forming a long hogback of Laramie sandstone on the park's west side.

A variety of wildlife passes through Ute Valley Park, including large mammals like black bears, bobcats, coyotes, and red foxes, as well as rabbits, ground squirrels, and raccoons. When hiking in summer, watch for rattlesnakes. They're common throughout the park, especially on Rattlesnake Ridge where they bask in the summer sun. Leash your dog and watch your children, especially if they scramble around on rocks where rattlers are often found. If you meet a rattlesnake, give it a wide berth, and leave the snake alone. Remember that you are an intruder in their home.

Beginning at the Piñon Valley Park Trailhead on the southwest side of Ute Valley Park, this fine hike follows three trails along the airy crest of Rattlesnake Ridge and then

returns on Triple Treat, a popular track often used by mountain bikers. The hike follows a closed service road, a wide
rocky trail, and single-track dirt trails to explore the ridge's
rugged terrain. All the trails and junctions are well marked
with signposts, making route finding easy. Mountain bikes
share most of the trails at Ute Valley Park, so keep alert for
bikers behind you. Parts of the hike may be icy in winter, so
pack micro spikes and trekking poles for traction and safety.

Miles and Directions

0.0 Start at the Piñon Valley Park Trailhead on the left side of a
gate. Hike east up a steep hill on a dirt service road, passing the Ute Valley bouldering area.

0.15 Reach a flat area at a junction on top of the hill, a park
map, and a junction with the Triple Treat trail on the left
(GPS: 38.912598, -104.856125). Hike north on Triple Treat
between timber fences, gently climbing the wide rocky trail.

0.3 Meet a signed junction on the left with the Rattlesnake
Ridge Trail (GPS: 38.914480, -104.856122). Ascend this
trail through Gambel oaks and ponderosa pines to the crest
of the rocky ridge. Bend north and follow the trail along the
ridgeline, passing boulders and small cliffs. This trail section
offers superb views west of Pikes Peak and the Rampart
Range.

0.75 Reach a broken sandstone outcrop and a timber fence
(GPS: 38.918290, -104.858461). The ridge is closed
beyond this point to protect high-value wildlife habitat. Go
right here and follow the trail north as it gently descends the
eastern side of the rocky hogback.

1.05 Reach a signed T junction with the Valley View Trail on the
right. Turn right on this trail and hike southeast, slowly gain-
ing elevation and then dropping steeply to the east.

1.4 Reach a junction with Triple Treat (GPS: 38.917490, -104.857018) and go right on it. Hike south on the wide trail, stepping over rocks, dodging mountain bikers, and gently climbing.

1.6 Reach a rocky area and meet a junction on the left with Nachos (GPS: 38.914715, -104.856119), a trail that heads east. Continue straight on Triple Treat, passing the first junction with the Rattlesnake Ridge Trail and dropping down to the top of the hill.

1.8 Reach the hilltop, trail map, and closed road. Go right on the road and descend steeply to the southwest.

1.95 Arrive back at the trailhead (GPS: 38.911278, -104.858175).

16 Ute Valley Park: BeaUTEiful Loop

This superb hike threads through a serene ponderosa pine forest and crosses open meadows on the southern edge of Ute Valley, making a perfect outing on a sunny Colorado day.

Start: South Rockrimmon Trailhead
Distance: 2.75 miles
Hiking time: About 1.5 hours
Type of hike: Lollipop loop
Trail names: BeaUTEiful Loop, Black and Blue Loop Trail
Difficulty: Easy. Cumulative elevation gain is 207 feet.
Trail surface: Paved trail at start, dirt trail, rocky in sections
Best season: Mar through Nov; parts of trail can be icy in winter.
Other trail users: Mountain bikers
Restrictions: Park hours are 5 a.m. to 9 p.m. Nov through Apr, 5 a.m. to 10 p.m. May through Oct. Leashed dogs allowed; pet waste must be picked up by the pet owner. Stay on designated trails. No littering, alcoholic beverages, smoking, camping, dumping, tree cutting, or fires. No e-bikes or other motorized devices, including power scooters, hoverboards, electric skateboards, ATVs, motorcycles, and remote-control vehicles.
Maps: Colorado Springs Parks, Recreation and Cultural Services website; USGS Pikeview
Trail contact: Colorado Springs Parks, Recreation and Cultural Services, (719) 385-5940

Finding the trailhead: From I-25, take exit 148 and drive west on South Rockrimmon Boulevard for 0.5 mile, then turn left (south) on Ute Valley Trail and drive 0.3 mile to a roundabout. Drive around it and take the third exit into a large parking lot and the South Rockrimmon Trailhead on the west side of the lot. GPS: 38.914940, -104.836871

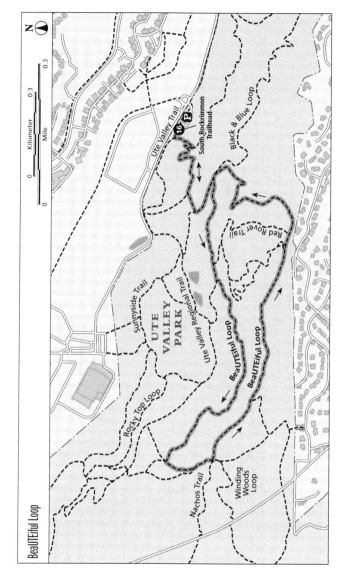

BeaUTEiful Loop

The Hike

Ute Valley Park spreads across 538 acres of foothills terrain, including a high hogback, sandstone bluffs, broad Ute Valley, open grasslands, and piney woods in northwest Colorado Springs. Four trailheads access the park's network of trails, attracting hikers, mountain bikers, and equestrians.

This excellent hike follows the BeaUTEiful Loop trail, named for the ancestral Utes who roamed the area, through a sun-dappled woodland of ponderosa pine and Gambel oak, open meadows studded with wildflowers in summer, and a rocky ridge with views of Pikes Peak and the Rampart Range. Signposts and directional arrows mark the trail at all junctions, so it is easy to stay on track.

Beginning at the South Rockrimmon Trailhead on the northeast side of Ute Valley Park, the hike first follows a section of the Black and Blue Loop, a popular mountain bike ride. At a signed junction, it joins the counterclockwise BeaUTEiful Loop, which is hiked back to the junction with the Black and Blue Loop. Follow it to the trailhead.

Parts of the hike are used by mountain bikers, who are supposed to yield to hikers. Keep watch for any bikers who don't slow down. Also, watch for rattlesnakes in Ute Valley from May to October. The north-facing slopes of the hike often hold snow and ice during the winter. Bring trekking poles and micro spikes for traction and balance.

Miles and Directions

0.0   Start at the South Rockrimmon Trailhead at a kiosk with a map and park info on the west side of the parking lot. Walk west on a paved trail, leaving the pavement and crossing the Ute Valley Regional Trail (GPS: 38.915103,-104.837257).

0.05 Reach a junction with a post signed BBL (Black and Blue Loop) and an arrow pointing left to "BeaUTEiful Loop." Go left on the Black and Blue Loop and follow the single-track trail through pines.

0.1 Reach a junction on the left with the Black and Blue Loop at a switchback (GPS: 38.914527, -104.837784). Keep right on the signed Black and Blue Loop and follow switchbacks west. Pass a rock flood-control levee and hike west.

0.3 Reach a junction and go left on the signed Black and Blue Loop trail (GPS: 38.914716, -104.839698). Descend laid stones, cross the bottom of a wash, and climb the other side. Continue on the Black and Blue Loop, passing a junction on the right with the Sunnyside Trail at 0.35 mile. Follow the Black and Blue Loop left and head east up the wide trail.

0.45 Reach a major junction with the "BeaUTEiful Loop" going sharp right and the Black and Blue Loop keeping left (GPS: 38.913839, -104.839100). This is the start of the loop. Go right on the BeaUTEiful Loop and hike through open ponderosa pine woods on a north slope.

0.65 Meet a junction on the left with the Red Rover Trail. Continue straight on the BeaUTEiful Loop.

0.7 Pass a junction on the right with a connector trail to the Ute Valley Regional Trail. The trail twists through quiet woods and grassy meadows on the southern slopes of Ute Valley.

1.25 Reach a signed junction (GPS: 38.915377, -104.850936) and go left on the BeauUTEifil Loop trail. Hike south up the wide trail.

1.35 Reach a four-way junction (GPS: 38.913816, -104.850846) and go left on the signed BeaUTEiful Loop. A right turn is the Nachos Trail and straight is the Winding Woods Loop, which leads to the Piñon Valley Park Trailhead to the west. Hike east on the BeaUTEiful Loop, gently climbing through a pine and Gambel oak forest and past a junction on the right. Watch for mountain bikes on this trail section. As the trail gains elevation, the terrain becomes rocky. Look west for good views of Pikes Peak.

1.85 As the trail reaches the park's southern boundary near houses, meet a junction on the left with a downhill mountain bike area and a connector on the right that goes to Golden Hills Road. Continue straight.

1.9 Reach a junction at a fence on the left (GPS: 38.911276, -104.841406) with Red Rover. Keep right on the BeaUTEiful Loop. No downhill bike travel is allowed on Red Rover. The next hike section descends north on the BeaUTEiful Loop, threading through rocks and terrain eroded by downhill bikers and then leveling out in open woods. Use caution if careless mountain bikers are on the trail.

2.28 Meet a junction with the Black and Blue Loop on the right (GPS: 38.913792,-104.838873). Keep left on the signed BeaUTEiful Loop.

2.3 Reach the junction at the start of the BeaUTEiful Loop trail and the end of the loop (GPS: 38.913836, -104.839038). Go right on the Black and Blue Loop trail and descend back down to the wash. Continue past the rock levee and climb northeast through pine woods.

2.75 Arrive back at the trailhead (GPS: 38.914940, -104.836871).

17 Blodgett Open Space: Dry Creek, Red Squirrel, Wagon Wheel, and Wildflower Trails

Combining four trails, this hike climbs through a shady pine and fir forest to a wide grassy ridge that offers spacious views of Blodgett Peak, the Rampart Range, and the foothills on the northwestern edge of Colorado Springs.

Start: North Blodgett Trailhead
Distance: 1.7 miles
Hiking time: 1 to 2 hours
Type of hike: Lollipop loop
Trail names: Dry Creek Loop, Red Squirrel Trail, Wagon Wheel Trail, Wildflower Trail
Difficulty: Moderate. Cumulative elevation gain is 555 feet.
Trail surface: Single-track dirt path
Best season: Mar through Nov; trail can be icy and muddy in winter.
Other trail users: Mountain bikers
Restrictions: Park hours are 5 a.m. to 9 p.m. Nov through Apr, 5 a.m. to 10 p.m. May through Oct. Leashed dogs allowed; pet waste must be promptly picked up and disposed of by the pet owner. Stay on designated trails. Park in designated areas and parking lots.

No littering, alcoholic beverages, smoking, camping, dumping, tree cutting, or fires. No e-bikes or other motorized devices, including power scooters, hoverboards, electric skateboards, ATVs, motorcycles, and remote-control vehicles.
Maps: Colorado Springs Park, Recreation and Cultural Services website map; USGS Cascade, Pikeview
Trail contacts: Colorado Springs Parks, Recreation and Cultural Services, (719) 385-5940; Pike National Forest, Pikes Peak Ranger District, (719) 636-1602

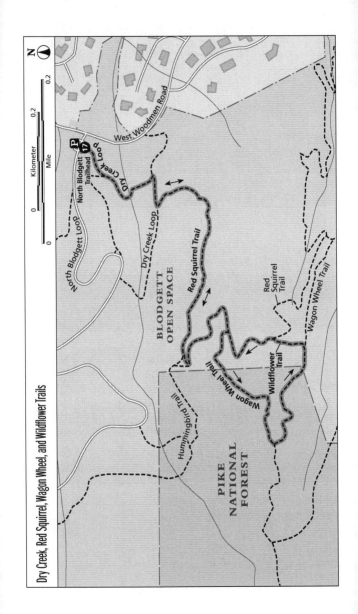

Dry Creek, Red Squirrel, Wagon Wheel, and Wildflower Trails

N

Kilometer
0   0.2
Mile
0   0.2

North Blodgett Loop

P
17
North Blodgett Trailhead

Dry Creek Loop

West Woodmen Road

Dry Creek Loop

BLODGETT OPEN SPACE

Red Squirrel Trail

Red Squirrel Trail

Wagon Wheel Trail

Hummingbird Trail

Wagon Wheel Trail

Wildflower Trail

PIKE NATIONAL FOREST

Finding the trailhead: From I-25, take exit 146 onto Garden of the Gods Road. Drive west on Garden of the Gods Road for 1.1 miles to Centennial Boulevard and turn right on it. Drive north on Centennial, passing Vindicator Drive, for 4.7 miles to a parking lot and the North Blodgett Trailhead on the left. Parking lot address: 3786 West Woodmen Road. GPS: 38.948924, -104.886278

The Hike

Blodgett Open Space, spreading across 384 hilly acres on the northwestern edge of Colorado Springs, offers a network of trails for hikers between West Woodmen Road and Pike National Forest. The trails, ranging from easy to moderate in difficulty, are well marked with signposts at junctions, ascend gradual grades, give fine views across the city below, and access unmaintained trails in the national forest, including a steep route to the summit of 9,436-foot Blodgett Peak.

The open space forms an interface between suburbs and the abrupt eastern flank of the Rampart Range. Terrain, ranging from 6,800 feet to over 8,200 feet at the northwest corner, includes drainages and slopes clad with mixed-conifer forest and ridgelines covered with oak thickets and dry grassland.

Besides providing recreational opportunities, the open space provides critical habitat for wildlife, including common mammals like black bear, mule deer, and coyote and over eighty foothills bird species. Bighorn sheep and peregrine falcons also live here. Parts of the open space, including the upper section of the described hike, were burned in the 2012 Waldo Canyon Fire. While the area is recovering, use caution around dead trees, especially on windy days.

Beginning at the North Blodgett Trailhead, this hike follows four trails up north-facing slopes blanketed with pine, fir, and spruce to a high loop across meadows and through dense Gambel oak groves before returning down to the trailhead. The trailhead has toilets, an information kiosk with a park map, and limited parking. Additional parking is in a designated strip along the west side of West Woodmen Road both north and south of the parking lot.

Miles and Directions

0.0 Start at the North Blodgett Trailhead on the southwest corner of the parking lot next to a park sign. Hike southwest on the Dry Creek Loop across a sunny grassy slope.

0.04 Reach a junction with the Dry Creek Loop's return trail on the right. Keep straight on the Dry Creek Loop, signed "To Red Squirrel Trail." Dip across a gulch and walk through open pine woods.

0.12 Meet a T junction and go right on the Dry Creek Loop toward the Red Squirrel Trail.

0.15 Reach a junction with the Red Squirrel Trail (GPS: 38.947449, -104.887596). Go left on it and gently climb south through open woods, then bend west and climb steeply through a mixed conifer forest.

0.45 Reach a junction with the Hummingbird Trail on the right. Keep left on the Red Squirrel Trail, signed "To Wagon Wheel Trail." Reach a switchback and go left above a steep slope to an open ridge and a sign explaining the 2012 Waldo Canyon Fire and its impact here.

0.6 Arrive at a junction on the right with the Wagon Wheel Trail and the start of the hike's loop section (GPS: 38.946092, -104.890646). Go right on the Wagon Wheel Trail. The left trail is the return route. Follow the Wagon Wheel Trail west along a wide ridge through a pine and fir forest and grassy meadows studded with Gambel oak groves. Stop for good views north to rocky Blodgett Peak.

0.65 Leave the open space and enter Pike National Forest on the unmaintained trail. Continue west toward the mountain front.

0.9 Reach the western end of the loop at an unsigned junction (GPS: 38.945209, -104.893382) and go left on the trail. The unnamed trail west of the junction climbs to the crest of the Rampart Range. Follow the left trail and gently descend meadows past the national forest–open space boundary.

0.96 Reach a junction with the Wildflower Trail on the left and follow this short connector trail north.

1.0 Arrive at a junction with the Red Squirrel Trail (GPS: 38.945212, -104.890805) and go left on it, crossing a meadow and dipping into a wash.

1.1 Reach the end of the loop at the junction with the Wagon Wheel Trail on the left. Continue straight on the Red Squirrel Trail and descend onto north-facing slopes.

1.25 Reach the junction with the Hummingbird Trail and go right.

1.55 Meet the T junction of the Red Squirrel Trail and Dry Creek Loop. Go right on the Dry Creek Loop and hike east on the wide trail.

1.58 Reach a junction and go left on the Dry Creek Loop. Follow it down and past the first junction with the Dry Creek Loop. Continue across an open slope toward the parking lot.

1.7 Arrive back at the trailhead (GPS: 38.948924, -104.886278).

18 Austin Bluffs Open Space: Pulpit Valley Loop

This easy hike forms a loop through Pulpit Valley, a serene enclave for wildlife and picturesque views, in a fragmented open space parkland in northern Colorado Springs.

Start: North Pulpit Rock Trailhead

Distance: 1.6 miles

Hiking time: About 1 hour

Type of hike: Lollipop loop

Trail names: Pulpit Rock Regional Trail, Pulpit Valley Loop

Difficulty: Easy. Cumulative elevation gain is 144 feet.

Trail surface: Dirt trail

Best season: Year-round

Other trail users: Mountain bikers

Restrictions: Park hours are 5 a.m. to 9 p.m. Nov through Apr, 5 a.m. to 10 p.m. May through Oct. No dogs allowed. Stay on designated trails. Park in designated parking lots. No littering, alcoholic beverages, smoking, camping, dumping, tree cutting, or fires.

Maps: Colorado Springs Parks, Recreation and Cultural Services website; USGS Pikeview

Trail contact: Colorado Springs Parks, Recreation and Cultural Services, (719) 385-5940

Finding the trailhead: From I-25, take exit 149 and drive east on Woodmen Road for 0.2 mile. Turn right on Campus Drive and go south to a roundabout and take the second exit onto Vincent Drive. Continue south and after 0.5 mile reach Dublin Boulevard. Turn right on Dublin, which turns into North Nevada Avenue, and drive south for 0.6 mile, then turn left into the Pulpit Rock Trailhead parking lot. The trailhead is on the southeast side of the lot. Street address: 5985 North Nevada Avenue. GPS: 38.918584, -104.813849

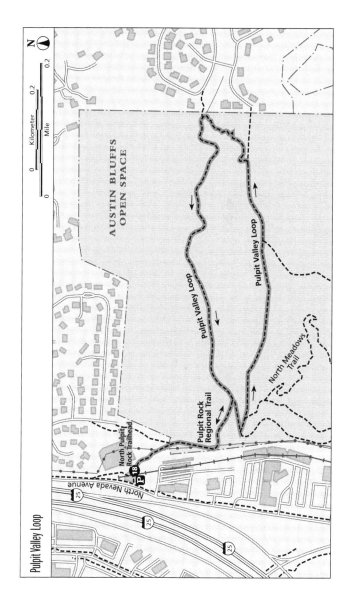
Pulpit Valley Loop

The Hike

This hike winds through Pulpit Valley, a wide drainage bordered by rocky bluffs on the north and 6,593-foot Pulpit Rock, an iconic Colorado Springs landmark, on the south. The gleaming stone fortress dominates northern Colorado Springs, towering above bustling I-25, the city's north–south thoroughfare. The hike and rock nestle within Pulpit Rock Park, part of the 584-acre Austin Bluffs Open Space on the city's north side. This protected parkland encompasses mesas, bluffs, and valleys east of North Nevada Avenue, forming a valuable scenic area and vital wildlife habitat, and serves as a crucial buffer from development.

Beginning at the North Pulpit Rock Trailhead, the hike makes a lollipop loop with gentle hills, a wide footbed, and spectacular views of Pulpit Rock and Pikes Peak. Passing through grasslands, thickets of Gambel oak, and riparian vegetation including tall cottonwood trees, the trail offers diverse scenery. Clear signage and directional arrows mark all trail junctions for easy navigation. While the hike's first segment is noisy with highway traffic, it quiets down as you hike east on the trail. During warmer months, be vigilant for rattlesnakes on the trail.

An intermittent creek flows down the drainage, passing beneath eroded banks, exposed pipes, and various concrete structures. The drainage has experienced severe downcutting and erosion, resulting in unstable embankments as high as 30 feet. Do not venture close to the edge, especially on the east section of the trail, since it can crumble beneath your feet.

Miles and Directions

0.0 Start at the North Pulpit Rock Trailhead and hike south on the wide Pulpit Rock Regional Trail. Descend a hill to the bottom of the valley, cross a bridge over an intermittent creek, and bend east across a hillside.

0.25 Reach a junction with the Pulpit Valley Loop on the left (GPS: 38.916291, -104.811822). This is the return trail. Go right on the Pulpit Rock Regional Trail / Pulpit Valley Loop and hike west toward college dorms.

0.3 Reach a junction with the signed Pulpit Valley Loop (GPS: 38.916111, -104.812762) and go left on it past a junction on the right with the North Meadows Trail. Hike east across a sloping grassy bench on the south side of the valley with Pulpit Rock rising to the east.

0.5 Pass another junction on the right with the North Meadows Trail and continue east 0.1 mile to a second junction with it. Cross meadows studded with Gambel oak groves. The trail moves closer to the creek encased in a deep canyon. Keep clear of the edge of dirt cliffs to the left; they regularly break off and fall into the creek. Descend to the creek, step across it on boulders, and climb the north bank.

0.85 Reach a junction with a spur trail that goes east to Spurwood Drive (GPS: 38.917077, -104.803519) and go left on the Pulpit Valley Loop. Hike west on the wide trail, gently descending a grassy bench north of the creek and its canyon. Cross the trickling creek at a concrete shelf and climb to the first junction.

1.35 Reach the Y junction at the end of the loop and go right on the signed Pulpit Rock Regional Trail. Descend to the bottom of the valley, cross a bridge over the creek, and climb the hill north toward the parking lot.

1.6 Arrive back at the trailhead (GPS: 38.918584, -104.813849).

19 Palmer Park: North Cañon, Templeton, and Edna Mae Bennett Nature Trails Loop

This excellent loop hike climbs North Cañon to a winding trail bordered by colorful sandstone bluffs and hoodoos at Palmer Park.

Start: North Cañon Trailhead
Distance: 1.9 miles
Hiking time: 1 to 2 hours
Type of hike: Loop
Trail names: North Cañon Trail, Templeton Trail, Edna Mae Bennett Nature Trail
Difficulty: Moderate. Cumulative elevation gain is 348 feet.
Trail surface: Single-track and double-track dirt path
Best season: Year-round; trail can be icy and muddy in winter.
Other trail users: Mountain bikers, equestrians
Restrictions: Park hours are 5 a.m. to 9 p.m. year-round. Gates at both park entrances on Paseo Road are locked at 9 p.m. Leashed dogs allowed; pet waste must be promptly picked up and disposed of by the pet owner. Stay on designated trails. Park in designated areas and parking lots. No littering, alcoholic beverages, smoking, camping, dumping, tree cutting, or fires.
Maps: Colorado Springs Parks, Recreation and Cultural Services website map; USGS Pikeview
Trail contact: Colorado Springs Parks, Recreation and Cultural Services, (719) 385-5940

Finding the trailhead: From I-25, take the Fillmore Street exit (exit 145). Drive east on Fillmore Street, which becomes North Circle Drive past the Union Boulevard intersection, for 2.5 miles to Paseo Road. Turn left onto Paseo Road and drive 0.8 mile northwest past a golf

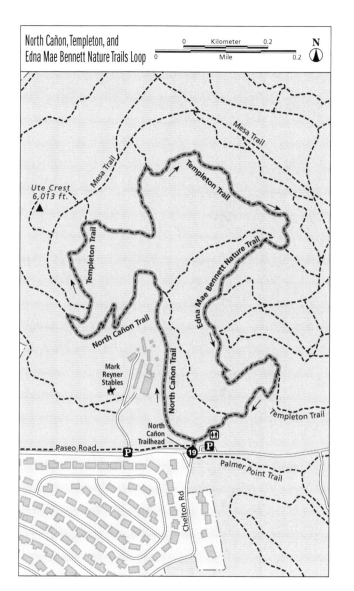

North Cañon, Templeton, and
Edna Mae Bennett Nature Trails Loop

0   Kilometer   0.2

0   Mile   0.2

N

Mesa Trail

Mesa Trail

Templeton Trail

Ute Crest
6,013 ft.

Templeton Trail

Edna Mae Bennett Nature Trail

North Cañon Trail

Mark
Reyner
Stables

North Cañon Trail

Templeton Trail

North Cañon
Trailhead

Paseo Road

19

Palmer Point Trail

Chelton Rd

course. Immediately after passing the gated park entrance, turn left into a parking lot at the North Cañon Trailhead (GPS: 38.877615, -104.777917). If the lot is full, additional parking is on the east side of Chelton Road south of the trailhead.

Alternatively, reach the trailhead from the park entrance on Maizeland Road 0.1 mile west of Academy Boulevard. Turn north on Paseo Road and drive 1.5 miles through Palmer Park to the trailhead on the right.

The Hike

This lovely loop hike, following the North Cañon, Templeton, and Edna Mae Bennett Nature Trails, lies in the northern sector of 730-acre Palmer Park in north-central Colorado Springs. The hike threads up North Cañon and then follows the crest of a rocky bluff that offers marvelous views across Colorado Springs to Pikes Peak before dipping down a ravine to the trailhead. Climbing high above houses, the hike explores shallow canyons, crumbling sandstone buttresses, and fanciful hoodoos shaped like primitive sculptures. The trails are easy to follow, with metal posts at trail junctions and arrows pointing the way. Parts of the hike cross rocks and sandy bedrock. While most of Palmer Park's 25 miles of trails are multiuse, you won't compete with mountain bikers on the hike—it's too darn rocky.

Today's parkland was originally settled by Matt France, who sold the area to Henry Austin, a sheep rancher, in 1872. He lent his name to a series of low hills called Austin Bluffs that stretches northeast from here to Pulpit Rock. In 1902 William Jackson Palmer, the founder of Colorado Springs, donated 692 acres to the city as a natural park.

Palmer Park, surrounded by suburbs and busy roads, remains a wooded enclave of Douglas firs on shady slopes, ponderosa pines, and thickets of Gambel oak, and a home for wildlife, including mule deer and rattlesnakes. The park is a popular destination for hiking, mountain biking, horseback riding, and picnicking and offers facilities such as a dog park, an off-leash dog area, a playground, picnic areas, softball and soccer fields, and a riding stable. A scenic drive, following Paseo Road, twists through the park to view points and trailheads.

The hike begins at the North Cañon Trailhead on Palmer Park's west side. Seasonal restrooms are at the trailhead. Head north on the North Cañon Trail past the Mark Reyner Trail to a junction with the Edna Mae Bennett Nature Trail, a loop trail named in memory of Edna Mae Bennett, a school-teacher who developed a nature-based curriculum for local children. She loved hiking in the North Cañon area, so after her death in 1972, her friends built the trail to honor Bennett's legacy. The second half of the hike follows that trail.

Go left on the signed North Cañon Trail and climb west to the Templeton Trail. Go right on the Templeton Trail and follow rimrock, dipping across drainages and passing fanci-ful formations, to a junction with the Bennett Trail. The cobblestone trail surface here was originally laid by Civilian Conservation Corps (CCC) workers in the 1930s. Go right and follow the Bennett Trail, which shares the next hike seg-ment with the Templeton Trail. Continue along the bluff's rim south and then east.

For the last leg, drop to a junction with the Templeton Trail. Keep right on the Edna Mae Bennett Nature Trail and descend to a sharp right turn. Scramble left here across bed-rock to an overlook below cliffs and an interesting cave to the south. The small grotto corkscrews into the cliff, forming a unique chamber that kids love to explore.

Miles and Directions

0.0 From the trailhead on Paseo Road left of the North Cañon parking lot, go straight on the signed Palmer Point Trail. Cross a bridge to a junction.

0.05 Reach a T junction and go left on the North Cañon Trail. Follow the wide trail northwest through meadows and Gambel oak groves.

0.25 Reach a three-way junction at an open area and go left on the North Cañon Trail (GPS: 38.880660, -104.778988). Straight ahead at the junction is the start of the Edna Mae Bennett Nature Trail. It finishes at the right trail. Follow the North Cañon Trail across a dry wash and switchback up the rocky trail on the east-facing slope above.

0.55 Reach a T junction near the mesa top (GPS: 38.880301, -104.781603) and go right on the Templeton Trail for the next leg.

0.6 Pass a junction on the left with a connector to the Mesa Trail and then another at 0.75 mile.

0.85 Pass an overlook on flat bedrock that looks south down North Cañon. Continue along the rimrock on the Templeton Trail.

0.95 Continue to a Y junction and keep right on the Templeton Trail.

1.35 Reach a signed junction with the Edna Mae Bennett Nature Trail on the right (GPS: 38.881871, -104.776169). Keep left on the Templeton Trail, which it shares with the Edna Mae Bennett Trail for the next leg. Follow the trail south and east along the rim of the bluff, with good views across Colorado Springs.

1.45 Pass a junction with a connector trail on the left signed for the Yucca Trail. Continue straight.

1.55 Pass another junction with a connector trail to the Lower Yucca Trail. Continue straight on the Templeton Trail and begin gently descending.

1.7 Reach a Y junction (GPS: 38.879151, -104.775730) and keep right on the Edna Mae Bennett Nature Trail. The Templeton Trail goes left. Descend the rocky trail.

1.75 Reach a sharp right turn (GPS: 38.878624, -104.776016) and continue hiking down the steep, rocky trail. Left of the turn is an amphitheater and shallow cave tucked into a sandstone cliff.

1.85 Reach a junction signed "To North Cañon Trailhead." Turn left on the trail and head downhill past restrooms. The Edna Mae Bennett Nature Trail continues straight from the junction and returns to its starting point.

1.9 Arrive back at the trailhead (GPS: 38.877615, -104.777917).

20 Fox Run Regional Park: Fallen Timbers Trail

The Fallen Timbers Trail winds through a mature ponderosa pine woodland in Fox Run Regional Park, an El Paso County parkland on the southwestern fringe of the Black Forest region.

Start: Fox Run Regional Park Trailhead
Distance: 1.5 miles
Hiking time: About 1 hour
Type of hike: Loop
Trail name: Fallen Timbers Trail
Difficulty: Easy. Cumulative elevation gain is 205 feet.
Trail surface: Dirt trail
Best season: Apr through Oct. Winters are often cold and snowy. Bring micro spikes and trekking poles for traction and balance.
Other trail users: Mountain bikers, equestrians
Restrictions: Park hours are 5 a.m.

to 9 p.m. Stay on designated trails. Leashed dogs allowed; pet waste must be picked up by the pet owner. Park in designated parking lots. No littering, alcoholic beverages, marijuana, smoking, camping, dumping, hunting, tree cutting, fires, fireworks, overnight parking, or discharge of firearms.
Maps: Fox Run Regional Park map on El Paso County website; USGS Monument
Trail contact: El Paso County Parks, (719) 520-7529

Finding the trailhead: From I-25, take exit 155 onto North Gate Road and drive east. From a roundabout just east of I-25, drive 1.7 miles and turn left onto Old North Gate Road. Drive 1.1 miles to a four-way stop at Roller Coaster Road and turn left on Roller Coaster. Drive north for 2.3 miles to the Fox Run Regional Park Trailhead and a dirt parking lot on the left. The trailhead is on the north side of

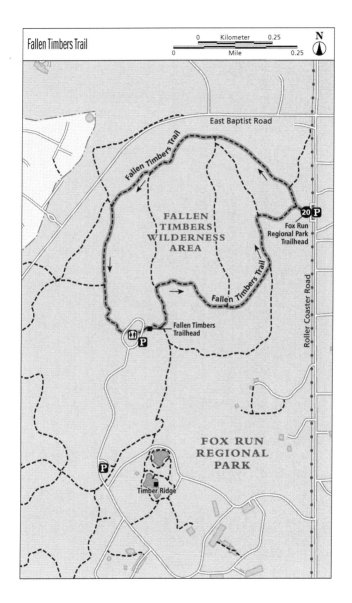

Fallen Timbers Trail

East Baptist Road

Fallen Timbers Trail

FALLEN
TIMBERS
WILDERNESS
AREA

Fallen Timbers Trail

20 P
Fox Run
Regional Park
Trailhead

Roller Coaster Road

Fallen Timbers
Trailhead

FOX RUN
REGIONAL
PARK

Timber Ridge

Kilometer
Mile
0   0.25

N

the parking lot. Trailhead address: 15926 Roller Coaster Road. GPS: 39.068095, -104.785384

The Hike

Following the Fallen Timbers Trail, this outstanding hike encircles the Fallen Timbers Wilderness Area, the undeveloped northern section of Fox Run Park on the west side of the Black Forest. The wide trail, shaded by a mature ponderosa pine forest, has gentle slopes, clearly marked junctions, and plenty of peace and quiet.

Fox Run Regional Park, a 417-acre El Paso County parkland, is a popular spot for outdoor fun in northern El Paso County. The park offers 4 miles of multiuse hiking trails, two small lakes, five picnic pavilions, playing fields, an off-leash dog area, and two playgrounds. Most visitors use the Oak Meadows Area and Pine Meadows Area with their developed facilities. Timber Ridge features Spruce Lake, Aspen Lake with a wedding gazebo, and a picnic area. Restrooms are scattered throughout the park.

The official trailhead for the Fallen Timbers Trail lies at the end of a dirt road north of Timber Ridge. The trailhead, however, is open seasonally and the access road closes during the winter. Hikers can park at a lot west of the lakes and hike 0.3 mile up the road to the trailhead in the off-season.

To avoid the closure, this described hike begins at the year-round Fox Run Regional Park Trailhead on Roller Coaster Road. The trailhead has a large parking lot and restrooms. The hike makes a counterclockwise loop on the Fallen Timbers Trail.

Miles and Directions

0.0 Start at the trailhead on the west side of the parking lot off Roller Coaster Road. Walk west past restrooms.

0.02 Reach a junction with the Fallen Timbers Trail and go right. Hike northwest through a ponderosa pine forest.

0.25 Reach a junction at the park's north end (GPS: 39.070357, -104.788986). Continue southwest on the main trail. Near the junction is a tall ponderosa pine tree that sprouted in 1846.

0.55 Meet a junction on the right with a connector trail to Baptist Road (GPS: 39.068272, -104.793088). Continue straight on the main trail.

0.7 Reach a junction on the right with an unnamed trail that goes to the park's south end. Keep left on the main trail and hike southeast through pine woods.

0.8 Arrive at a road that loops around the official Fallen Timbers Trailhead (GPS: 39.064537,-104.792599). Cross the road and follow a timber-lined trail around a restroom (open seasonally) to the road on its east side. Cross the road and walk to the trailhead by a parking lot.

0.85 Reach the trailhead on the road's east side (GPS: 39.064663, -104.791704) and hike east.

0.9 Reach a junction and go left on the Fallen Timbers Trail. Hike north to a high point and bend left. Descend southeast.

1.15 Reach a junction on the left (GPS: 39.065333, -104.788565). Continue straight on the main trail, hiking east and then north to a high point. Turn left here and descend northeast on wooded slopes.

1.48 Reach the junction with the trail to the parking lot. Turn right and walk toward the lot.

1.5 Arrive back at the trailhead (GPS: 39.068095, -104.785384).

21 Santa Fe Open Space: Ranch Road, Far View Trail, and Burlington Trail Loop

This easy hike follows an old railroad bed to a lollipop loop on three trails that thread through meadows and an oak and pine woodland on the south slope of cliff-lined Ben Lomand Mountain near Palmer Lake.

Start: Santa Fe Trailhead
Distance: 2.9 miles
Hiking time: About 1.5 hours
Type of hike: Lollipop loop
Trail names: New Santa Fe Regional Trail, Ranch Road, Far View Trail, Burlington Trail
Difficulty: Easy. Cumulative elevation gain is 116 feet.
Trail surface: Single-track dirt path
Best season: Mar through Nov; trail can be icy or muddy in winter.
Other trail users: Mountain bikers
Restrictions: Trail hours are 5 a.m. to 9 p.m. Apr through Oct, 6 a.m. to 6 p.m. Nov through Mar. Leashed dogs allowed; pet waste must be picked up by the pet owner. Stay on designated trails. Park in designated areas and parking lots. No littering, alcoholic beverages, smoking, camping, dumping, tree cutting, or fires.
Maps: El Paso County Parks website; USGS Palmer Lake
Trail contact: El Paso County Parks and Recreation, (719) 520-7529

Finding the trailhead: From Colorado Springs, drive north on I-25 and take exit 163 onto County Line Road. Drive west on County Line Road for 2.6 miles and turn left into the Palmer Lake Regional Recreation Area just before railroad tracks and Spruce Mountain Road on the north side of Palmer Lake. Drive south for 0.2 mile on a dirt road on the west side of the lake to the road's end and a parking lot. The trailhead is right of restrooms on the south side of the lot. The trailhead is also reached from Monument by driving north on CO 105 to County Line Road. Trailhead address: 199 County Line Road, Palmer Lake. GPS: 39.123427, -104.910467

The Hike

This lollipop loop hike twists through open meadows, Gambel oak groves, and a ponderosa pine woodland in the 65-acre Santa Fe Open Space, an untouched slice of ranchland tucked against the rugged south flank of Ben Lomand Mountain. Lying east of the quaint town of Palmer Lake, the open space preserves a foothills environment, providing important wildlife habitat and expansive views south of Mount Herman and the Rampart Range. A conservation easement protected the land in 2003 and then El Paso County purchased it in 2017 from the McGuire/Close family, descendants of the land's early settlers, to protect its conservation values.

Beginning at the Santa Fe Trailhead in the 26-acre Palmer Lake Regional Recreation Area, a parkland on the east side of the town of Palmer Lake that includes its namesake lake, the hike follows the New Santa Fe Regional Trail. This 14-mile-long trail, part of the American Discovery Trail, follows the abandoned railbed of the Atchison, Topeka and Santa Fe Railroad south from Palmer Lake through the Air Force Academy.

The wide trail swings southeast around 7,644-foot Ben Lomand Mountain, which forms the Palmer Divide, a long ridge that divides the Arkansas River and South Platte River watersheds. Ragged cliffs, composed of coarse Dawson arkose, line the mountain's southern escarpment above the

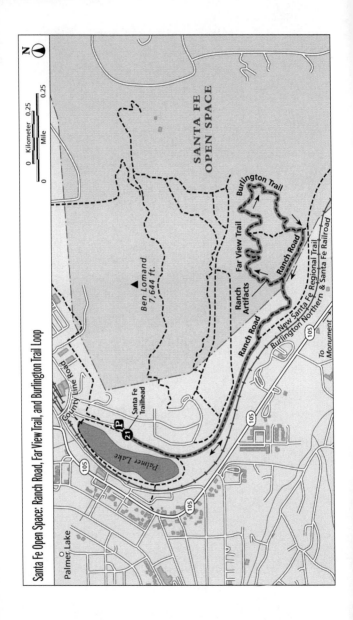

Santa Fe Open Space: Ranch Road, Far View Trail, and Burlington Trail Loop

N

0   Kilometer   0.25

0   Mile   0.25

SANTA FE
OPEN SPACE

Burlington Trail

Far View Trail

Ranch Artifacts

Ranch Road

Ben Lomand
7,644 ft.

Ranch Road

New Santa Fe Regional Trail
Burlington Northern & Santa Fe Railroad

105

To
Monument

105

County Line Road

Santa Fe
Trailhead

21

Palmer Lake

Palmer
Lake

105

hike. At a sign, the hike leaves the New Santa Fe Regional Trail and follows three trails—Ranch Road, Far View Trail, and Burlington Trail—through the open space, returning to the starting point at the old railbed.

Expect views across the southern Front Range, watch for wildlife, and leave no trace of your passage. Points of interest along the hike include a trailside display of ranch artifacts, including farm machinery and a rusted 1953 Dodge Coronet Suburban once owned by rancher Herman Kyle. From the trail's high point on a ridge, look east to Elephant Rock, a large formation with an arch that forms the elephant's trunk. While the rock lies within a conservation easement, the area is not open to public access. After completing the loop through the open space, return to the trailhead on the New Santa Fe Regional Trail.

Miles and Directions

0.0 Start at the Santa Fe Trailhead at the south end of the parking lot on the east side of the lake. Hike south on the wide trail past a playground.

0.15 Reach a junction with a trail on the right (GPS: 39.121105, -104.911788). Keep straight on the main trail.

0.65 Reach a junction on the left with a sign for the Santa Fe Open Space and a park map (GPS: 39.117234, -04.905240). Go left on Ranch Road and follow the single-track trail across a meadow with views north to ruddy cliffs lining the south slope of 7,644-foot Ben Lomand Mountain and then through pine woods.

0.9 Reach a junction with the signed Far View Trail (GPS: 39.116111, -104.901799). Go left on it and hike 0.05 mile to a ranch artifact display with an old car and rusted machinery. Continue through Gambel oak groves and scattered mines.

1.3 Descend a hill to a signed junction with the Burlington Trail (GPS: 39.117716, -104.899177). Continue straight on the Burlington Trail and hike through a mixed oak and pine forest.

1.8 Reach a signed T-junction with the Far View Trail (GPS: 39.115892, -104.899025). Go left on Far View and hike south through woods.

1.85 Reach a junction on the right with Ranch Road (GPS: 39.115216, -104.898971). Go right on it to finish the loop. *Option:* If you want to return on the New Santa Fe Regional Trail, continue straight on the Far View Trail for 80 feet and go right.

2.0 Arrive at the start of the loop at the junction of Ranch Road and the Far View Trail. Continue straight on Ranch Road.

2.25 Reach the junction with the wide New Santa Fe Regional Trail and go right to return to the trailhead and parking lot.

2.9 Arrive back at the trailhead (GPS: 39.123427, -104.910467).

22 Pike National Forest: Red Rocks Trail

The Red Rocks Trail rises through aspens and ponderosa pines to an eroded wonderland of twisted sandstone formations north of Woodland Park.

Start: "Alternate Red Rocks Trailhead"
Distance: 1.2 miles
Hiking time: About 1 hour
Type of hike: Lollipop loop
Trail names: "West Red Rocks Trail," Red Rocks Trail (#708)
Difficulty: Easy. Cumulative elevation gain is 214 feet.
Trail surface: Dirt trail
Best season: May through Oct. Winters are snowy. Park at winter trailhead off CO 67.
Other trail users: Mountain bikers, equestrians

Restrictions: Leashed dogs allowed; pet waste must be picked up and disposed of by the pet owner. Stay on designated trails. Park in designated areas and parking lots. No littering, alcoholic beverages, smoking, camping, dumping, tree cutting, or fires. No toilets at the trailhead.
Map: USGS Mount Deception
Trail contact: Pike National Forest, Pikes Peak Ranger District, (719) 636-1602

Finding the trailhead: From the junction of US 24 and CO 67 on the west side of Woodland Park, turn right on CO 67 and drive north for 3.9 miles. Turn right on FR 355 and park at the alternative trailhead just east of CO 67. (The official Red Rocks Trailhead is 0.3 mile farther east on FR 355 on the right.) GPS: 39.04395, -105.08007

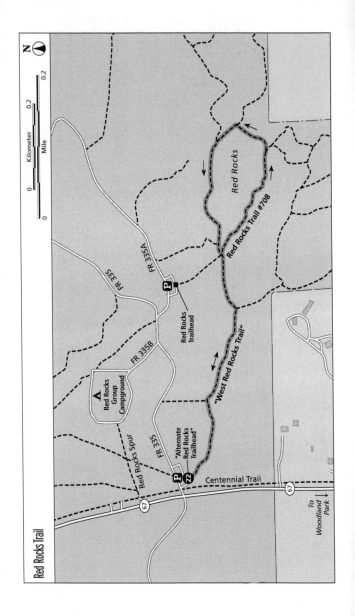

Red Rocks Trail

The Hike

The "West Red Rocks Trail" and Red Rocks Trail gently climb from a trailhead at 8,114 feet off CO 67 through an open ponderosa pine woodland to a geologic oddity—a cluster of sandstone formations rising above the forest that appear transplanted from the famed Garden of the Gods. Surrounded by ancient granite, the rocks are Fountain Formation sandstone and conglomerate deposited over 300 million years ago as sediment below the eastern foot of the Ancestral Rocky Mountains.

Over eons of weathering, the gentle touches of water and ice eroded the ruddy sandstone outcrops into bizarre shapes, with deep crevices, shallow caves, sharp spires, standing hoodoos, and rounded buttresses in two major formations. These form a playground for exploration. Be cautious when scrambling above the ground since the sandstone is friable and edges and pebbles break frequently, and remember that it's always easier to climb up than to descend.

The hike begins at an alternative trailhead just after the turnoff from CO 67 and follows the unofficially named "West Red Rocks Trail." The signed Forest Service trailhead is almost a half-mile farther east on FR 355A, but starting there considerably shortens the hike. The first section follows the West Red Rocks Trail through an aspen grove and over a rounded ridge to the red rock formations. The second segment makes a counterclockwise loop on the Red Rocks Trail around the rocks through a ponderosa pine and Douglas fir woodland.

The trail on the south side of the rocks is steep in a couple spots as it climbs to the trail high point at 8,323 feet and is not well defined, intersecting with a network of social trails. None of the trail junctions are signed, so follow the Miles and Directions to stay on track. The Red Rocks Trail is open year-round but snow and ice cover it in winter, so bring micro spikes and trekking poles.

Miles and Directions

0.0 Start at the "Alternate Red Rocks Trailhead" on the south end of a parking lot off CO 67. Hike east on the "West Red Rocks Trail" through an aspen glade, then climb an open ridge and gently descend east.

0.25 Pass a junction on the right.

0.35 Reach a junction on the left with the Red Rocks Trail from the official Red Rocks Trailhead and the return trail (GPS: 39.043058, -105.073818). Keep right on the trail and head southwest toward the red rocks.

0.45 Reach another junction west of the red rocks and hike toward the rocks and then around their right side. Follow the trail around the first rock group to a cove, then continue southeast up a short hill and hike past the south side of the second group and the trail high point. Descend a hill to a defined trail and hike northeast.

0.6 Reach a T junction (GPS: 39.042737, -105.070240) and go left on a good trail. Hike northwest past a junction at 0.65 mile.

0.8 Reach a junction with a wide trail. Continue west on level ground.

0.85 Reach the first junction with the trail from the second trail-head at a big pine tree. Hike west on the trail, easily climbing over the blunt ridge and descending northwest.

1.2 Arrive back at the trailhead (GPS: 39.04395, -105.08007).

23 Manitou Park Recreation Area: Manitou Lake Trail

The Manitou Lake Trail is an easy trail that encircles Manitou Lake north of Woodland Park. It's an ideal hike for families and children, with easy grades, nature study, and scenic views of Pikes Peak.

Start: Manitou Lake Trailhead
Distance: 0.8-mile loop
Hiking time: About 1 hour
Type of hike: Loop
Trail name: Manitou Lake Trail (#670)
Difficulty: Easy. Cumulative elevation gain is 16 feet.
Trail surface: Dirt path and boardwalk
Best season: Mar through Nov; trail may be icy, snowpacked, or muddy in winter.
Other trail users: Hikers only

Restrictions: Open year-round, weather permitting. Day-use fee required. No motorboats, swimming, or wading. Fishing and non-motorized boating allowed. Vault toilets, potable water, and picnic tables available. Reserve picnic pavilion at recreation.gov.
Map: USGS Mount Deception
Trail contact: Pike National Forest, Pikes Peak Ranger District, (719) 636-1602

Finding the trailhead: From Colorado Springs and I-25, drive west on US 24 to Woodland Park. Turn north on CO 67 on the west side of Woodland Park and drive 7.8 miles to Manitou Park Recreation Area. Turn right (east) into the area and park in the first or second parking lot. The trailhead is opposite the vault toilets. Allow 45 minutes to drive from Colorado Springs to the trailhead. GPS: 39.089962, -105.098447

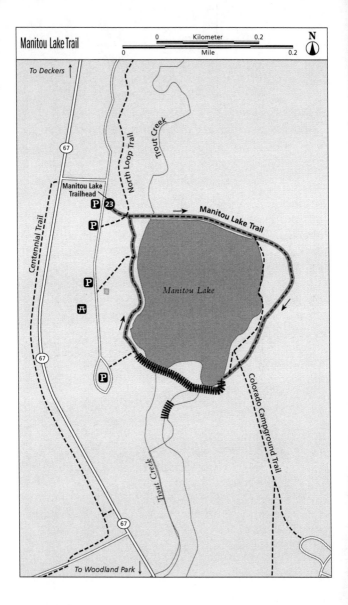

The Hike

Manitou Park Recreation Area, administered by Pike National Forest, stretches along CO 67 north of Woodland Park and includes several campgrounds and trails. A fun, easy day hike follows the Manitou Lake Trail (#670) around the perimeter of scenic 5-acre Manitou Lake, offering superb views of snowcapped Pikes Peak to the south, bird-watching with a variety of songbirds and waterfowl, and fishing in the placid trout-stocked lake. Hand-paddled craft like canoes are allowed on the lake, but swimming, wading, and motorboats are not permitted. The easy nature trail is partly accessible for strollers and wheelchairs, although it may be impassable when wet or muddy.

Begin at the Manitou Lake Trailhead opposite the vault toilets at the first parking lot. The hike goes clockwise around Manitou Lake. Cross a footbridge over the dam's spillway and walk east atop an earthen dam built in 1937 to a trail fork. Keep left and then go right and hike south through a ponderosa pine grove and a meadow east of the lake. At the lake's south end, the trail crosses an elevated boardwalk through a marsh, with thick stands of cattails providing habitat for birds, including red-winged blackbirds, great blue herons, and kingfishers. Interpretive signs describe the importance of wetlands. Continue north along the west shoreline of the lake beneath shady pines and past a wheelchair-accessible fishing ramp to return to the trailhead.

Other trail adventures in the recreation area include the North Loop Trail (#670), a lollipop loop that begins by the trailhead and strolls north alongside Trout Creek, and the Colorado Campground Trail (#670B), which heads south from the Manitou Lake Trail to Colorado Campground and then joins the Centennial Trail (#669) to South Meadows Campground and on to Woodland Park.

Miles and Directions

0.0 Start at the trailhead east of the first parking lot at the northwest end of the lake. After 160 feet, reach a junction with the return loop on the right and the North Loop Trail on the left. Continue east and cross the bridge above the dam and spillway. Continue east across the top of an earthen dam.

0.1 Reach a junction at the east end of the earthen dam. Keep left on the main trail and continue to the dam's end, then go right and hike south through meadows and pines. The right fork drops down to the lake edge, providing fishing access.

0.4 Pass a junction with the Colorado Campground Trail (#670B) on the left and continue southwest on the Manitou Lake Trail (GPS: 39.087207, -105.095361). Walk across a boardwalk over wetlands at the lake's south end.

0.5 At the boardwalk's end, bend north on the dirt trail and hike along the lake's western shoreline.

0.8 Arrive back at the trailhead (GPS: 39.089962, -105.098447).

24 Mueller State Park: Grouse Mountain Overlook Trail

This fun hike climbs to the 9,851-foot summit of "Grouse Mountain" and a spectacular overlook that offers panoramic views of Pikes Peak and cliffs and valleys in Mueller State Park.

Start: Grouse Mountain Trailhead
Distance: 1.0 mile
Hiking time: 30 minutes to 1 hour
Type of hike: Out and back
Trail names: Cheesman Ranch Trail (#17), Grouse Mountain Overlook Trail (#16)
Difficulty: Moderate. Cumulative elevation gain is 153 feet.
Trail surface: Single-track and double-track dirt path
Best season: May through Oct; trail is icy and snowy in winter.
Other trail users: First trail section open to mountain bikers and equestrians
Restrictions: Fee area. Open year-round. The trail is closed June 1–20 for elk calving. The last road section through Grouse Mountain Campground closes from mid-Oct to mid-May, requiring a 0.5-mile hike on the road to the trailhead. Day-use hours are 5 a.m. to 10 p.m. Visitor center hours are 9 a.m. to 4 p.m. No dogs on trails. Stay on designated trails; do not short-cut trails. No motorized vehicles on trails. No backcountry camping or fires. Respect natural and historic features; do not collect rocks, artifacts, flowers, or antlers.
Maps: Trail map at park website; USGS Divide
Trail contact: Mueller State Park, (719) 687-2366

Finding the trailhead: From the Cimarron Street / US 24 exit (exit 141) in Colorado Springs, drive west on US 24 up Ute Pass and through Woodland Park. Continue west on US 24 to the town of

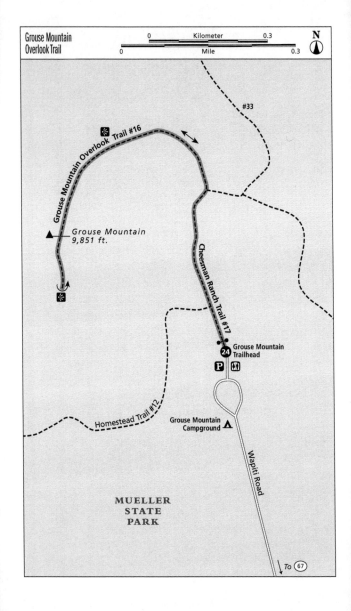

Divide. Turn left (south) onto CO 67 toward Cripple Creek. Drive south for 3.8 miles to the park entrance and turn right (west) into the park. After paying the entrance fee, follow Wapiti Road past the visitor center and through the campground to a large parking lot at the Grouse Mountain Trailhead at the road's end. Start the hike at the trailhead at the north end of the lot. Restrooms are in the parking area. GPS: 38.902401, -105.183225

The Hike

The Grouse Mountain Overlook Trail (#16) climbs to the rocky summit of unofficially named "Grouse Mountain," the highest point in Mueller State Park. The trail offers leisurely hiking with a gradual grade and a spacious summit with views of Pikes Peak and the park's shaggy hills and valleys, and distant vistas of snow-covered mountains. Families and kids enjoy the hike and reaching the mountain summit. The wide trail is easy to follow and designated with trail markers at every junction. The trail closes from June 1 to 20 every year for elk calving.

The hike starts at the Grouse Mountain Trailhead at the northern end of the park road and campground. A kiosk at the trailhead displays a map, park rules, and information about black bears, which are common in the park. Begin by hiking north on the Cheesman Ranch Trail (#17), passing through a gate to an interpretive sign about the park's habitats and animals. It continues past a junction with the Homestead Trail to a junction and the start of the overlook trail.

The Grouse Mountain Overlook Trail (#16) gently climbs through a mixed conifer and aspen forest interspersed with open meadows. The trail from here is for hikers only; no mountain bikes or horses are allowed. The double-track trail climbs through a spruce and fir forest floored with mountain juniper. Glades of quaking aspen and meadows spill down the mountain's east flank. After a short ascent you reach the mountain's humped summit and splendid views of the northeast flank of Pikes Peak, with dark forests ending at timberline.

For the best views, hike south from the summit to a lower point. This single-track trail threads along a ridge, descending through boulder gardens to a twisted dead tree and an outcrop of granite boulders. Sit on a stone and enjoy the expansive view. To the southeast tower Pikes Peak and conical Sentinel Point. Farther south rises pyramid-shaped Mount Pisgah above the historic mining town of Cripple Creek. The sawtoothed Sangre de Cristo Range, with nine 14,000-foot peaks, stretches against the southwestern sky. Look west across the wooded hills of Mueller State Park to the distant Sawatch Range poking above the horizon. After enjoying the vista, return down the trail.

Miles and Directions

0.0 Start at the Grouse Mountain Trailhead at the north end of the park road in Grouse Mountain Campground. Hike north on the Cheesman Ranch Trail (#17) for 100 feet to a junction with the Homestead Trail (#12) on the left. Continue straight on the Cheesman Ranch Trail.

0.2 Reach a junction with the Grouse Mountain Overlook Trail (#16) and go left on it. Follow the trail up north-facing slopes.

0.4 Reach the signed summit of Grouse Mountain (GPS: 38.903800, -105.186014). Hike south on the trail through boulders.

0.5 Reach an overlook on the south side of the Grouse Mountain summit. After admiring views of Pikes Peak and Raspberry Mountain to the southeast, hike back over the summit and descend the trail.

1.0 Arrive back at the trailhead (38.902401, -105.183225).

25 Mueller State Park: School Pond Trail

This excellent hike threads through mature conifer forests, crosses open grasslands, and descends to the still waters of School Pond before climbing to a high ridge and mountain views.

Start: School Pond Trailhead
Distance: 1.6 miles
Hiking time: 30 minutes to 1 hour
Type of hike: Lollipop loop
Trail names: School Pond Trail (#2), Aspen Trail (#21)
Difficulty: Easy. Cumulative elevation gain is 312 feet.
Trail surface: Single-track and double-track dirt path
Best season: May through Oct; trail is snowpacked and icy in winter. Bring cross-country skis, snowshoes, or micro spikes and trekking poles.
Other trail users: Mountain bikers, equestrians

Restrictions: Fee area. Open year-round. Day-use hours are 5 a.m. to 10 p.m. Visitor center hours are 9 a.m. to 4 p.m. No dogs on trails. Sign in and out of register at trailhead. Stay on designated trails; do not shortcut trails. No motorized vehicles on trails. No backcountry camping or fires. Respect natural and historic features; do not collect rocks, artifacts, flowers, or antlers.
Maps: Trail map at park website; USGS Divide
Trail contact: Mueller State Park, (719) 687-2366

Finding the trailhead: From the Cimarron Street / US 24 exit (exit 141) in Colorado Springs, drive west on US 24 up Ute Pass and through Woodland Park. Continue west on US 24 to the town of Divide. Turn left (south) onto CO 67 toward Cripple Creek. Drive south for 3.8 miles to the park entrance and turn right (west) into the park.

From the turnoff, drive west on Wapiti Road for 1.3 miles, passing the entrance and self-service fee station and the Dragonfly Children's Nature Trail to a signed left turn to the School Pond Trailhead and parking lot. Start the hike at the trailhead at the lot's south end. GPS: 38.878697, -105.176301

The Hike

The School Pond Trail forms a picturesque loop through the southeast corner of Mueller State Park, winding through grassy meadows, wooded hillsides, and an open ridge with picture-perfect views of Pikes Peak and pointed Sentinel Point. Starting at the trailhead on Wapiti Road, the hike is clearly marked by posts with trail numbers and arrows. The hike follows the School Pond Trail (#2) and part of the Aspen Trail (#21).

Midway on the trail is serene School Pond, the hike's main attraction. Originally built as a stock pond during the park's ranching days, the glassy pond reflects sky and clouds. A bench beside the pond makes a scenic lunch spot. The pond area offers fine wildlife watching for mule deer and elk, particularly in the morning and evening.

Mueller State Park spreads across 5,112 rugged acres with an average elevation of 9,600 feet on the west side of 14,109-foot Pikes Peak. The park offers 55 miles of hiking on forty-four trails that explore its valleys, ridges, and mountains. The trails, some open to mountain bikers and equestrians, lead to scenic overlooks with far-ranging views of the Sangre de Cristo Mountains and wooded valleys floored with trickling creeks and ponds. The park is renowned as the premier wildlife-watching area in the Pikes Peak region, with a diversity of mammals including black bear, elk, and

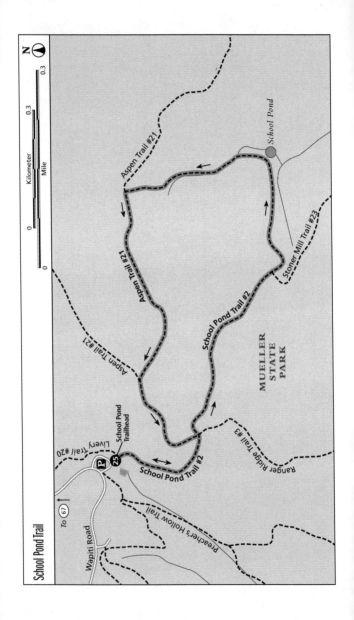

School Pond Trail

N

Kilometer
0.3   0.3
Mile
0   0.3

To 67

Wapiti Road

Livery Trail #20

P

25

School Pond Trailhead

School Pond Trail #2

Preacher's Hollow Trail

Aspen Trail #21

Aspen Trail #21

Aspen Trail #21

School Pond Trail #2

School Pond Trail #2

Ranger Ridge Trail #3

Stoner Mill Trail #23

School Pond

MUELLER STATE PARK

mule deer and over 115 bird species. The park's sheer size and lack of roads ensure seclusion and isolation. Mueller's amenities include 136 developed campsites, 4 backcountry campsites, 4 picnic areas, and a visitor center with displays and educational programs.

The park's web of trails can be linked together to form loop hikes of varying lengths and difficulty. Trails range from short and easy to long and challenging. Pick up a trail map when you enter the park or download a copy from the park's website to plan other foot adventures. Mueller State Park is also one of the best places near Colorado Springs for winter sports, including cross-country skiing, snowshoeing, and sledding, and winter camping.

Miles and Directions

0.0 Start at the School Pond Trailhead at the south side of the parking lot. Walk past a kiosk with a park map and pass the right side of a metal gate and a junction on the left with the Livery Trail (#20). Follow the wide School Pond Trail, a closed service road, south across wooded slopes.

0.19 Bend east and reach a four-way signed junction (GPS: 38.876773, -105.175542) with the Ranger Ridge Trail (#3) on the right, the School Pond Trail (#2) straight ahead, and the School Pond / Aspen Trail (#21) (the return trail) on the left. Go straight on the School Pond Trail and descend the old road/trail down a valley with grassy slopes on the left and woods on the right. As the trail drops, admire views southeast to Sentinel Point.

0.5 Reach a junction on the right with the Stoner Mill Trail (#23). Continue straight down the valley on the School Pond Trail.

0.65 Arrive at the north side of School Pond (GPS: 38.875076, -105.167837), a placid pond tucked in a valley. Sit on a bench and enjoy the view, then continue hiking on the trail, curving left and climbing north up a long grassy valley.

0.9 Reach the crest of a wide ridge and a junction (GPS: 38.878391, -105.168598) with the signed Aspen Trail (also School Pond Trail). Go left on it and follow the old ranch road west on an open ridge through meadows and a mixed woodland of quaking aspen, Douglas fir, and ponderosa pine.

1.2 Reach a junction on the right with the Aspen Trail and the start of its loop. Continue straight on the Aspen / School Pond Trail, climbing a gentle hillside and then bending south. Descend to the first junction.

1.4 Return to the junction at the start of the School Pond Trail's loop (GPS: 38.876773, -105.175542) and go right on the School Pond Trail, hiking north across wooded slopes.

1.6 Arrive back at the trailhead (GPS: 38.878697, -105.176301).

26 Florissant Fossil Beds National Monument: Ponderosa Loop Trail

This excellent, accessible trail loops through an open forest by the visitor center, passing educational signs that vividly bring the monument's fascinating fossil history to life.

Start: Visitor center trailhead
Distance: 0.42 mile
Hiking time: About 30 minutes
Type of hike: Loop
Trail name: Ponderosa Loop Trail
Difficulty: Easy. Cumulative elevation gain is 40 feet.
Trail surface: The first section is a concrete sidewalk. The trail surface is poly pavement with a granite crusher mix. Wheelchair accessible and accommodates electric and hand-powered wheelchairs. Surface hardness allows for wheelchair tires and walkers. Gentle grades and wide enough for two chairs to pass.
Best season: Apr through Oct; snow and ice often cover the trail in winter.
Other trail users: Hikers only
Restrictions: Fee area. Park hours

are 9 a.m. to 4:30 p.m. After-hours access is prohibited. Trails are day-use only. No dogs or other pets on trails or in backcountry, except in pet exercise area, picnic area by visitor center, and on paved roads in the park. Do not leave pets unattended in vehicles. No campfires, bicycles, motorized vehicles, hunting or discharge of firearms, camping, or drones. Do not remove or disturb any fossils, rocks, antlers, or other natural or cultural items.
Maps: Florissant Fossil Beds National Monument website; USGS Lake George
Trail contact: Florissant Fossil Beds National Monument, (719) 748-3253

Finding the trailhead: From I-25 and downtown Colorado Springs, take the Cimarron Street / US 24 exit (exit 141) and drive west for

35 miles, passing through Woodland Park and Divide, to the town of Florissant. Turn left (south) onto CR 1 and drive 2 miles to the visitor center road. Turn right (west) and drive 0.2 mile to a parking area at the visitor center. The trailhead is on the west side of the visitor center. GPS: 38.913716, -105.285600

The Hike

The Ponderosa Loop is an accessible ADA-compliant trail that allows hikers with mobility issues to explore the monument's fossil wonders and a ponderosa pine forest. The trail caters not only to seniors and families with small children, but also to visitors short on time, acclimating to the 8,500-foot elevation, or wanting a leisurely hike.

The self-guided trail, lined with interpretive signs, is fully wheelchair accessible and wide enough so two wheelchairs can pass safely. The gentle gradient allows for both electric and hand-powered chairs, and the trail's surface accommodates tires on wheelchairs and walkers. The surface is poly pavement with a crushed granite mix that looks natural. The first and last section of the hike west of the visitor center follows a concrete sidewalk. Opening in 2006, the trail allows hikers of all abilities to experience and enjoy Florissant Fossil Beds. Snow often covers the trail in winter, making it inaccessible to wheelchairs.

Start your fossil hike at the west door of the visitor center. You can pick up a trail map and look at fossils, including small leaf and insect fossils, and watch an informative film.

The hike first follows the Ponderosa Loop Trail counterclockwise, beginning at a shelter that protects the stumps of petrified redwood trees that flourished here over 30 million years ago. Follow the concrete trail to the first stump and

Ponderosa Loop Trail

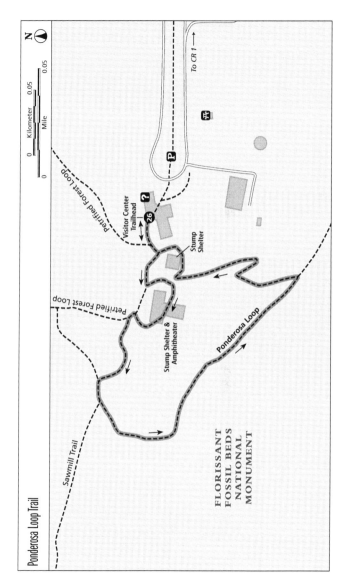

N

Kilometer
0   0.05

Mile
0   0.05

To CR 1

Petrified Forest Loop

Visitor Center
Trailhead

26

Stump Shelter

Petrified Forest Loop

Stump Shelter &
Amphitheater

Ponderosa Loop

Sawmill Trail

**FLORISSANT
FOSSIL BEDS
NATIONAL
MONUMENT**

continue to the next stump pavilion for interesting exhibits and two large redwood stumps, including the Redwood Trio, three stumps rising from a common root system.

Past the shelter, follow the paved trail to a Y junction and go left on the smooth Ponderosa Loop. A signpost points the way. The short hike offers educational signs, benches, and a couple buried stumps. The rock-lined double-track trail crosses a gentle hillside covered with fir, spruce, and pine. At the only trail junction, keep left on the wide trail and return to the first stump shelter.

For more trail adventures, the monument offers a non-motorized, all-terrain wheelchair with beefy, inflatable tires for more-difficult trails like the Petrified Forest Loop or an out-and-back hike on the level section of the Boulder Creek Trail. Call ahead to reserve the unit and borrow it for the day.

Miles and Directions

0.0 Begin at the trailhead at the west door of the visitor center. Go west on the concrete trail for 90 feet to a junction north of the first stump shelter and go right. The left trail is the return route. Walk west for another 90 feet.

0.01 Reach a junction at the northeast corner of the second shelter and turn left. Follow the paved trail through the shelter, stopping to read interpretive signs and admire the Redwood Trio and another large stump. Leave the shelter and go north to rejoin the concrete trail and go left.

0.1 Reach a Y junction at the end of the paved trail and go left on the trail signed "Ponderosa Loop Accessible Trail." Meet a junction on the right with a spur to the Petrified Loop and continue straight.

0.15 Reach a junction and go left on the signed Ponderosa Loop (GPS: 38.914070, -105.287254). This is the start of the hike's loop section. Hike south and southeast through woods on the rock-lined trail, passing benches and signs about life zones, habitat changes, the role of fire, and animals.

0.3 Reach a junction on the right with the signed Sawmill Loop and Hans Loop trails (GPS: 38.912613, -105.286110) and go sharply left. Gently descend north to a switchback and then another switchback. To the right is a petrified stump with a tree growing from it. Continue north on the trail.

0.38 Meet the paved trail on the second stump shelter's east side (GPS: 38.913522, -105.286134) and go right. Follow the sidewalk around the south side of the first shelter and reach the first junction. Go right toward the visitor center.

0.42 Arrive back at the trailhead (GPS: 38.913716, -105.285600).

27 Florissant Fossil Beds National Monument: Petrified Forest Loop

This excellent hike explores Florissant Fossil Beds' ancient fossil record, passing petrified redwood stumps and old quarries that have unearthed some of the world's finest fossilized insects, including butterflies and leaves.

Start: Visitor center trailhead
Distance: 1.05 miles
Hiking time: About 1 hour
Type of hike: Loop
Trail names: Ponderosa Loop, Petrified Forest Loop
Difficulty: Easy. Cumulative elevation gain is 84 feet.
Trail surface: Dirt trail; paved at the hike's start
Best season: Apr through Nov; trail may be snow-covered in winter.
Other trail users: Hikers only
Restrictions: Fee area. Park hours are 9 a.m. to 4:30 p.m. After-hours access is prohibited. Trails are day-use only. No dogs or other pets on trails or in backcountry, except in pet exercise area, picnic area by visitor center, and on paved roads in the park. Do not leave pets unattended in vehicles. No campfires, bicycles, motorized vehicles, hunting or discharge of firearms, camping, or drones. Do not remove or disturb any fossils, rocks, antlers, or other natural or cultural items.
Maps: Trail map available at monument visitor center; USGS Lake George
Trail contact: Florissant Fossil Beds National Monument, (719) 748-3253

Finding the trailhead: From I-25 and downtown Colorado Springs, take the Cimarron Street / US 24 exit (exit 141) and drive west for 35 miles, passing through Woodland Park and Divide, to the town of Florissant. Turn left (south) onto CR 1 and drive 2 miles to the visitor center road. Turn right (west) and drive 0.2 mile to a parking area at the visitor center. The trailhead is on the west side of the visitor center. GPS: 38.913716, -105.285600

The Hike

The Petrified Forest Loop explores the geological record preserved and protected at 5,998-acre Florissant Fossil Beds National Monument, a stone repository of ancient life. Like most of the monument's hikes, the trail begins at the visitor center. The trail offers fun and educational hiking with interpretive signs scattered along its length, giving insight into yesterday's fossil record and today's mountain ecosystems.

Nestled within Florissant Fossil Beds lies one of the world's premier fossil sites. Concealed beneath the meadows and woodlands is a vast repository of a lost world dating back some 34 million years ago. Here, fossils come in two types: the diminutive and the colossal. The petrified stumps and trunks of soaring redwood trees, entombed by volcanic mudflows that once dammed the valley and formed Lake Florissant, capture our imagination. Like the redwood forests of present-day California, the ancient giants at Florissant reached staggering heights of up to 300 feet.

However, it is the delicate fossils of tiny insects, animal and fish remnants, and fragments of plant life hidden within thin shale layers that distinguish the fossil beds. Florissant boasts an impressive array of over 1,500 insect species, including nearly all the fossilized butterflies found in the Western Hemisphere, as well as the only fossil of a tsetse fly, now indigenous to equatorial Africa.

Your fossil hike begins at the western entrance of the visitor center. Before heading out, pick up a trail map; peruse the fossil displays, including small leaf and insect specimens; and enjoy a superb introductory film.

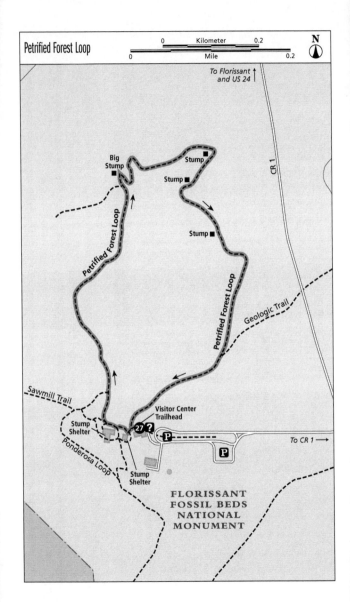

Petrified Forest Loop

0   Kilometer   0.2

0   Mile   0.2

N

To Florissant
and US 24

CR 1

Big
Stump

Stump

Stump

Petrified Forest Loop

Stump

Petrified Forest Loop

Geologic Trail

Sawmill Trail

Visitor Center
Trailhead

Stump
Shelter

27

P

To CR 1

Ponderosa Loop

Stump
Shelter

P

FLORISSANT
FOSSIL BEDS
NATIONAL
MONUMENT

The hike follows the Ponderosa Loop, an accessible trail, for its first segment. First, pass a stump shelter that protects the large stump of a *Sequoia affinis*, a close relative of today's coast redwood. Keep right on the concrete trail to another shelter that houses the famed Redwood Trio, three interconnected trunks stemming from a single base, and another large stump. The shelters shield the fragile stumps from weathering. Continue west until the paved trail ends at a fork. Go right on the marked Petrified Forest Loop and hike north.

The trail winds along the western edge of a broad valley, once the lakebed of ancient Lake Florissant, crossing meadows studded with glades of ponderosa pine. Interpretive signs are scattered along the trail, offering insights into fossils, ancient ecosystems, park geology, native peoples, and the area's colorful history.

Near the north end of the loop, the trail reaches the aptly named Big Stump. One of the monument's largest fossils, Big Stump is the remains of a massive redwood tree that was at least 230 feet high and over 750 years old when volcanic mud, or lahar, buried its base. In addition to the excavated stumps seen along the trail, remote sensing has revealed at least thirty more stumps that remain buried along the edge of the vanished lake. Most of the stumps remain underground to protect them.

After viewing the colorful stump, continue east on the trail, passing more stumps, to a hillock dotted with ponderosa pines. The trail bends right here and heads southwest back to the visitor center. Read signs that detail the area's early history, when competing fossil pits vied for customers who paid to view the stumps, dig fossils, and stay in large hotels. The hike ends on the west side of the visitor center.

Miles and Directions

0.0 Start at the trailhead on the west side of the visitor center. Hike west on the paved Ponderosa Loop past two stump shelters that protect petrified stumps.

0.05 Reach a Y junction at the end of the concrete trail and northwest of the second shelter. Go right on the signed Petrified Forest Loop (GPS: 38.913856, -105.286515). Hike north on the wide trail through ponderosa pines and meadows, passing several interpretive signs.

0.1 Pass a junction on the left with a spur trail that goes west to the Ponderosa Loop. Continue north.

0.4 Pass a closed junction with a trail to Scudder Pit and continue to Big Stump on the left (GPS: 38.918377, -105.286098). Admire the colorful stump and read nearby educational signs. Continue the hike by looping east past the site of an old hotel and cross the valley to a pine-covered hillock. Turn south and hike past several exposed stumps, including one that may be the largest petrified stump in the world with a diameter of 16 feet and a projected height of about 300 feet. Continue south on the trail.

0.9 Reach a junction on the left with the Geologic Trail (GPS: 38.915087, -105.283615). Read interpretive signs here, then continue southwest on the trail toward the visitor center.

1.05 Arrive back at the trailhead (GPS: 38.913716, -105.285600).

Appendix: Additional Information

Gear and Guidebook Retailers
Garden of the Gods Trading Post
324 Beckers Ln.
Manitou Springs, CO 80829
(719) 685-9045
www.gardenofthegodstradingpost.com

Mountain Chalet
15 North Nevada Ave.
Colorado Springs, CO 80903
(719) 633-0732
https://mtnchalet.com

REI Colorado Springs
1376 E. Woodmen Rd.
Colorado Springs, CO 80920
(719) 260-1455
https://www.rei.com/stores/colorado-springs

Management Agencies
Bear Creek Nature Center
245 Bear Creek Rd.
Colorado Springs, CO 80906
(719) 520-6387
https://communityservices.elpasoco.com/nature-centers/
bear-creek-nature-center

Cheyenne Mountain State Park
410 JL Ranch Heights Rd.
Colorado Springs, CO 80926
(719) 576-2016
https://cpw.state.co.us/state-parks/cheyenne-mountain
-state-park

Colorado Springs Parks, Recreation and Cultural Services
1401 Recreation Way
Colorado Springs, CO 80905
(719) 385-5940
https://coloradosprings.gov/PRCS

El Paso County Parks and Recreation
2002 Creek Crossing
Colorado Springs, CO 80905
(719) 520-7529
https://communityservices.elpasoco.com/parks-and-recreation/
el-paso-county-parks

Florissant Fossil Beds National Monument
PO Box 185
Florissant, CO 80816
(719) 748-3253
www.nps.gov/flfo

Fountain Creek Nature Center
320 Pepper Grass Ln.
Fountain, CO 80817
(719) 520-6745
https://communityservices.elpasoco.com/nature-centers/
fountain-creek-nature-center

Garden of the Gods Visitor & Nature Center
1805 N. 30th St.
Colorado Springs, CO 80904
(719) 634-6666
https://gardenofgods.com

Helen Hunt Visitor Center
North Cheyenne Cañon Park
(719) 633-5701
https://coloradosprings.gov/helenhuntfalls

Mueller State Park
PO Box 39
21045 CO 67 South
Divide, CO 80814
(719) 687-2366
https://cpw.state.co.us/state-parks/mueller-state-park

Pike National Forest
Pikes Peak Ranger District
601 S. Weber St.
Colorado Springs, CO 80903
(719) 636-1602
www.fs.usda.gov/psicc

Starsmore Visitor and Nature Center
North Cheyenne Cañon Park
2120 S. Cheyenne Canyon Rd.
Colorado Springs, CO 80906
(719) 385-6086
https://coloradosprings.gov/starsmore

About the Author

Stewart M. Green, a Colorado Springs native, hiked, climbed, photographed, and traveled across the American West and the world in search of memorable images and experiences to document. Based in the Springs, Stewart, a freelance writer and photographer for Globe Pequot Press, FalconGuides, and Every Adventure Publishing, wrote and photographed over sixty-five travel and outdoor adventure books, including *Scenic Driving Colorado*, *Rock Climbing Colorado*, *Best Hikes Colorado Springs*, *Hiking Colorado's Hidden Gems*, *Best Lake Hikes Colorado*, *Hiking Waterfalls Colorado*, *Climbing Pikes Peak*, and *Hiking Garden of the Gods*. His photographs and writing have been published in many magazines, books, websites, and ads. Before his death in 2024, he was writing a memoir of his early climbing days in Moab and Colorado and a historic time travel novel about Cripple Creek.

THE TEN ESSENTIALS OF HIKING

American Hiking Society

Whether you plan to be gone for a couple of hours or several months, make sure to pack these items. Become familiar with these items and know how to use them.

Find other helpful resources at AmericanHiking.org/hiking-resources.

1. Appropriate Footwear

6. Safety Items (light, fire, and a whistle)

2. Navigation

7. First Aid Kit

3. Water (and a way to purify it)

8. Knife or Multi-Tool

4. Food

9. Sun Protection

5. Rain Gear & Dry-Fast Layers

10. Shelter

FALCONGUIDES®

MAKE ADVENTURE YOUR STORY™

Since 1979, FalconGuides has been a trailblazer in defining outdoor exploration. Elevate your journey with contributions by top outdoor experts and enthusiasts as you immerse yourself in a world where adventure knows no bounds.

Our expansive collection spans the world of outdoor pursuits, from hiking and foraging guides to books on environmental preservation and rockhounding. Unleash your potential as we outfit your mind with unparalleled insights on destinations, routes, and the wonders that await your arrival.

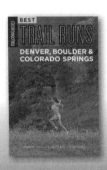